From
Resurrection
To
Pentecost

From Resurrection To Pentecost

Easter-Season Meditations

ROBERT F. MORNEAU

A Crossroad Faith & Formation Book
The Crossroad Publishing Company
New York

The poems of Ruth Mary Fox are reprinted here from *Some Did Return,*
published by Wake-Brook House, © 1976 by Ruth Mary Fox.

The poems by Anne Higgins, Ralph Wright, O.S.B., and Helen Fahrbach
have been reprinted here with the permission of the authors.

The Crossroad Publishing Company
370 Lexington Avenue, New York, NY 10017

Copyright © 2000 by Robert F. Morneau

Printed in the United States of America

Library of Congress Cataloging-in-Publication Data

Morneau, Robert F., 1938-
    From Resurrection to Pentecost : Easter-season meditations / Robert F.
Morneau.
        p. cm.
    Includes bibliographical references.
    ISBN 0-8245-1855-1 (alk. paper)
    1. Eastertide – Meditations. 2. Catholic Church – Prayer-books and
devotions – English.   I. Title.
BX2170.E25 M67   2000
242'.36 – dc21

99-050924

1   2   3   4   5   6   7   8   9   10   06   05   04   03   02   01   00

Contents

Walking the Road to Emmaus

Life holds for us those special, blessed moments of rich encounter when heart speaks to heart, when our separateness and self-importance is foregone, when communion through conversation is tasted. One such moment in the scriptures is the story of Jesus conversing with the two disciples as they walked toward Emmaus (Luke 24:13–35).

The story is a familiar one. Jesus is dead, crucified as a common criminal; the community of disciples is in disarray; two of them head back to their hometown of Emmaus but meet a stranger who explains all the events of the recent past. Invited to dinner, the stranger breaks bread and is recognized as the risen Lord. With hearts on fire, the disciples hurry back to Jerusalem to proclaim the good news of the resurrection.

The risen Lord continues to walk with all of us on our journey to Emmaus or Emmitsburg, to London or Calcutta, to Auckland or Seattle. If we are attentive to the "strangers" who cut across our path or who journey a few steps with us, we might well recognize some form of God's love and mercy in the conversation. It might even happen that our hearts will catch on fire. Then we become

the "stranger" to others and help them interpret their lives in the
light of God's love.

Many of the people we journey with come as a surprise. However, we can also select companions who have something to say,
some wisdom to impart. Why not, during the Easter season, travel
with a few poets. Though their language system is not that of
daily discourse, they do have a certain angle of vision that might
help us to see things a bit differently. Perhaps even their singing
with words might cause our heart to skip a beat or illumine our
mind to see a little more clearly or even cause our feet to walk
the path of peace. More, maybe a poem or two might ignite our
hearts with love and help us to give light and warmth to others.

Our journey is long and we need the sound of a human voice.
The disciples heard the voice of Jesus and recognized the speaker
in the breaking of bread. We too can be guided and consoled,
challenged and affirmed by the voice of our companions, poets or
otherwise. The main thing is that we must never travel alone.

There are seven weeks between Easter and Pentecost. This
volume of poems and ponderings offers one form of companionship for this season of the liturgical year. The format is direct
and simple: (1) identification of the day of the Easter season and
the Gospel reading (the reader is encouraged to spend five to ten
minutes meditating on the Gospel passage); (2) a brief contextual
comment on the Gospel; (3) a refrain (antiphon) taken from the
Divine Office summarizing a core idea in the Gospel (this can
be used as a mantra for one's prayer); (4) a selection of poetry to
read and reread out loud; (5) a commentary on the poem followed by three questions for personal or communal reflection;
(6) a concluding prayer taken from the Divine Office for that day.

As we journey from Easter to Pentecost our constant companion is the Holy Spirit. Jesus promised that the Spirit would be

with us always. So let me conclude this preface with a poem by the Carmelite Jessica Powers. This verse is a heartfelt plea that the Holy Spirit come into our lives with the gifts of life, light and love:

COME, SOUTH WIND

By south wind is meant
the Holy Spirit who awakens love.
St. John of the Cross

Over and over I say to the south wind: come,
waken in me and warm me!
I have walked too long with a death's chill in the air,
mourned over trees too long with branches bare.
Ice has a falsity for all its brightness
and so has need of your warm reprimand.
A curse be on the snow that lapsed from whiteness,
and all bleak days that paralyze my land.

I am saying all day to Love who wakens love:
rise in the south and come!
Hurry me into springtime; hustle the winter
out of my sight; make dumb
the north wind's loud impertinence. Then plunge me
into my leafing and my blossoming,
and give me pasture, sweet and sudden pasture.
Where could the Shepherd bring
his flocks to graze? Where could they rest at noonday?
O south wind, listen to the woe I sing!
One whom I love is asking for the summer
from me, who still am distances from spring.

Jessica Powers

From
Resurrection
To
Pentecost

EASTER SEASON

Week One

(Easter Week)

EASTER MONDAY

Matthew 28:8–15

T HE RISEN LORD'S COMMAND "Go and carry the news" flows down the ages. In every century the news of God's love and mercy revealed in the risen Christ is to be proclaimed so that people might experience the peace that comes only through the presence of the Spirit. There are other stories that reach our ears as well down through the generations: God is dead! Jesus is not risen! The Spirit doesn't exist! Yet women that come from an empty tomb, as well as prophets and poets and believers know otherwise.

Refrain: Go quickly and tell his disciples: The Lord is risen, alleluia.

GOD'S GRANDEUR

The world is charged with the grandeur of God.
It will flame out, like shining from shook foil;
It gathers to a greatness, like the ooze of oil
Crushed. Why do men then now not reck his rod?

Generations have trod, have trod, have trod;
And all is seared with trade; bleared, smeared with toil;
And wears man's smudge and shares man's smell: the soil
Is bare now, nor can foot feel, being shod.

And for all this, nature is never spent;
There lives the dearest freshness deep down things;
And though the last lights off the black West went
Oh, morning, at the brown brink eastward springs —
Because the Holy Ghost over the bent
World broods with warm breast and with ah! bright wings.

Gerard Manley Hopkins

God's grandeur is surely in creation: the giant redwoods of California, the rolling prairies of Nebraska, the vistas of the Rocky Mountains. But God's grandeur is even more manifest in the person of Jesus who redeemed all generations from sins of searing, smudging, blearing. Now all is new.

Much darkness covers the earth. Suffering and death daily remind us of the human condition. But the black West, with all its terror, is countered by the eastern morning. Deep, deep down in all things a freshness, a "dearest freshness," dwells, and because of this hope awakens.

And the cause of all this? Nothing less than the power of God's faithful Spirit brooding over our broken and fragile world. Cosmic vision here! A faith vision that brings warmth and light.

- *Where do you find God's grandeur in creation?*

- *How has our generation seared-bleared-smeared God's world?*

- *Have you visited lately your own place of "dearest freshness deep down things"?*

Praying with the Church

Father,
you give your Church constant growth
by adding new members to your family.
Help us put into action in our lives
the baptism we have received with faith.
We ask this through our Lord Jesus Christ, your Son,
who lives and reigns with you and the Holy Spirit,
one God, for ever and ever.

EASTER TUESDAY
John 20:11–18

W HY DO WE WEEP? Sometimes the tears flow because of self-pity — the loss of a friend or a season diminishes *us* and our sorrow is ultimately selfish. When grace is present and love courses through our being, our weeping is authentic grief for the suffering of another. Seldom is it simply one or the other. Our crying and laughing contain life's ambiguous coloring. Mary Magdalene wept and both the angels and the Lord asked why.

Refrain: Jesus called her by name: Mary. She turned to him and said: Rabboni. Then he said to her: Do not touch me; I have not yet ascended to my Father, alleluia.

SPRING AND FALL
to a young child

Margaret, are you grieving
Over Goldengrove unleaving?
Leaves, like the things of men, you
With your fresh thoughts care for, can you?
Ah! as the hearts grows older
It will come to such sights colder
By and by, nor spare a sigh
Though worlds of wanwood leafmeal lie;
And yet you will weep and know why.
Now no matter, child, the name:
Sorrow's springs are the same.
Nor mouth had, no nor mind, expressed
What heart heard of, ghost guessed:
It is the blight man was born for,
It is Margaret you mourn for.

Gerard Manley Hopkins

In early life, with our dreams and fresh thoughts dominant, any grieving will be mostly self-pity. The falling of leaves, the death of a pet, the departure of a playmate bring tears and sorrow, but they moisten only our hurting and parched souls.

Far different the grief of friends who have had life and love together. Far different is the grief when someone dies who has literally "saved" you. Then the weeping, no, sobbing, has little of self in it. The gravesite is visited in all weather regardless of the sacrifice.

Because of the resurrection and the grace of new life, the human "blight" of perpetual mourning only for ourselves has found a healing ointment. In Jesus, in his triumph over death and sin, we have good news to report: joy's springs are as much available as are the wells of sorrow. Joy flows from knowing our God as Father, Savior, and Sanctifier.

- *What have you grieved over in the past year?*

- *Where do your tears come from?*

- *What can keep our hearts from growing cold as we experience more and more loss in life?*

Praying with the Church

> Father,
> by this Easter mystery you touch our lives
> with the healing power of your love.
> You have given us the freedom of the sons of God.
> May we who now celebrate your gift
> find joy in it forever in heaven.
> Grant this through our Lord Jesus Christ, your Son,
> who lives and reigns with you and the Holy Spirit,
> one God, for ever and ever.

EASTER WEDNESDAY
Luke 24:13–35

O N THE ROAD TO EMMAUS the forlorn disciples caught sight of the risen Lord only after they heard how, in Jesus' death, the scriptures were fulfilled and only after the bread was broken. The cross, a symbol of death and failure, was now transformed into a sign of divine providence. The disciples' hearts were stirred to new life. The cross's brute beauty brought light and life into Calvary's darkness and death.

Refrain: Beginning with Moses and the prophets, Jesus interpreted for them all that had been written of him in the scriptures, alleluia.

THE WINDHOVER
To Christ our Lord

I caught this morning morning's minion, king-
    dom of daylight's dauphin, dapple-dawn-drawn Falcon, in
        his riding
    Of the rolling level underneath him steady air, and striding
High there, how he rung upon the rein of a wimpling wing
In his ecstasy! then off, off forth on swing,
    As a skate's heel sweeps smooth on a bow-bend: the hurl
        and gliding
    Rebuffed the big wind. My heart in hiding
Stirred for a bird, — the achieve of, the mastery of the thing!

Brute beauty and valour and act, oh, air, pride, plume here
    Buckle! and the fire that breaks from thee then, a billion
Times told lovelier, more dangerous, O my chevalier!

No wonder of it: sheer plod makes plough down sillion
Shine, and blue-bleak embers, ah my dear,
   Fall, gall themselves and gash gold-vermilion.

Gerard Manley Hopkins

The morning falcon is a splendid sight as it buffets the wind
in great mastery. It's enough to stir the heart to jealousy, certainly
admiration. Jesus took on the winds of suffering and death. In
the eyes of the faithless all seemed lost. But death was not to be
victorious. Jesus continued to be with the community, feeding it
with words and the bread of life.

Our hearts need tending. The fire there can be too easily ex-
tinguished. It is by pondering God's word (Word) that we again
see the beauty and valour and activity of God's Spirit in creation and in human exchange. Once our hearts embrace the
redemptive mystery of the cross and resurrection, they break forth
in great brilliance and glory.

There should be no surprise here, no cause for wonder. Just as
creaturely things like a plough or fire can, in their own mastery,
stir the heart by their excellence, so the faith vision of Jesus risen
and alive should fill our days with joy and love.

- *What causes your heart to stir?*

- *What gift has God given you that deserves mastery and
  sharing?*

- *Search the sky this week in search of a hawk.*

Praying with the Church

> God our Father,
> on this solemn feast you give us the joy of recalling
> the rising of Christ to new life.
> May the joy of our annual celebration
> bring us to the joy of eternal life.
> We ask this through our Lord Jesus Christ, your Son,
> who lives and reigns with you and the Holy Spirit,
> one God, for ever and ever.

EASTER THURSDAY
Luke 24:35–48

THERE ARE TWO CONTRASTING MOODS that continually occur during this Easter week. One is that of fear stemming from so many unknowns; the other is peace when the presence of the risen Lord is made manifest. Within seconds the hearts of the disciples are turned upside down: terrified and afraid for their very lives and then calmed of all anxieties as Christ breaks again and again into their lives.

Refrain: Jesus stood in the midst of his disciples and said: Peace be with you, alleluia.

PEACE

When will you ever, Peace, wild wooddove, shy wings shut,
Your round me roaming end, and under be my boughs?
When, when, Peace, will you, Peace? I'll not play hypocrite
To own my heart: I yield you do come sometimes; but
That piecemeal peace is poor peace. What pure peace allows
Alarms of wars, the daunting wars, the death of it?

O surely reaving Peace, my Lord should leave in lieu
Some good! And so he does leave Patience exquisite,
That plumes to Peace thereafter. And when Peace here does
      house
He comes with work to do, he does not come to coo,
   He comes to brood and sit.

Gerard Manley Hopkins

Peace is such an illusive quality. A deep sense of rightness in
relationships is shattered within a human breadth by our sins of
denial and betrayal. At the Last Supper the apostles experienced
Jesus' profound love. Too soon they would be filled with incredible terror. Peace, that "wild wooddove," knew not how to perch
in their souls.

Piecemeal peace is better than none, but yet it has its inherent
poverty. The soul wants total, abiding peace, an assurance that
nothing will cause it to flee. Such an expectation is not compat-
ible with the human condition. Pure peace awaits us only in our
full participation of the paschal mystery, in the risen life.

But there is a deep consolation here. Jesus gives us the Spirit
of patience to persevere in hope to endure adversity. The disciples
would be sent out to do their missionary work graced not with a
pure, whole peace but with exquisite patience which, in due time,

would become the fullness of God's peace and joy. Indeed, we are not left as orphans.

- *In what way is peace like a "wild wooddove"?*

- *Name some moments of piecemeal peace in your life.*

- *What is the connection between peace and patience?*

Praying with the Church

> Father,
> you gather the nations to praise your name.
> May all who are reborn in baptism
> be one in faith and love.
> Grant this through our Lord Jesus Christ, your Son,
> who lives and reigns with you and the Holy Spirit,
> one God, for ever and ever.

EASTER FRIDAY
John 21:1–14

WHEN THINGS HAPPEN three or more times a certain serious-ness sets in. Maybe there is something here that demands careful attention and possibly a major response. Jesus again breaks into the life of the apostles, who are resorting to their old trade of fishing. Again the Lord stirs their hearts into new life, into a new spring filled with promise and hope. Gathered around a morning fire and sharing the intimacy of food and conversation, the disciples experience the great mystery of the resurrection.

Refrain: This was the third time Jesus had shown himself to his disciples after he had risen from the dead, alleluia.

SPRING

Nothing is so beautiful as spring —
    When weeds, in wheels, shoot long and lovely and lush;
    Thrush's eggs look little low heavens, and thrush
Through the echoing timber does so rinse and wring
The ear, it strikes like lightnings to hear him sing;
    The glassy peartree leaves and blooms, they brush
    The descending blue; that blue is all in a rush
With richness; the racing lambs too have fair their fling.

What is all this juice and all this joy?
    A strain of the earth's sweet being in the beginning
In Eden garden. — Have, get, before it cloy,
    Before it cloud, Christ, lord, and sour with sinning,
Innocent mind and Mayday in girl and boy,
    Most, O maid's child, thy choice and worthy the winning.

Gerard Manley Hopkins

Few things are lovelier than nature bursting forth in newness of life. Wild flowers, the song of birds, the blooming trees, the blueness of the sky, the animals astir make springtime a season of incredible vitality. The throbbing of life is so tangible that only those who are blind and deaf fail to recognize the miracles of new life. Springtime speaks of creation and resurrection. Springtime draws us back to the garden of Eden and the gift of existence.

But that existence has been marred with sinning, a transgression so deep that for many life is now sour and distasteful. Jesus, through the mystery of the incarnation, plunges into our messy world and chooses to take on the fullness of the human condition, all things save sin. So prized is humankind that God sent his only son to win back all who have gone astray. No greater love. . . .

One wonders whether one of the disciples, after the fish had been hauled ashore and the charcoal fire was properly fueled and the fish and bread tasted, one wonders if one disciple might have whispered to another: "What is all this juice and all this joy?" Like racing lambs that have their fling, the apostles knew that grace called ecstasy. Jesus, the way and truth and light, was also the spring that gave life, life to the full.

- *What does springtime mean for you? What juices and joys do you experience?*

- *How do you keep the "vigil" of the mysteries of creation and resurrection?*

- *How many times has the Lord appeared to you? In what forms?*

Praying with the Church

> Eternal Father,
> you gave us the Easter mystery
> as our covenant of reconciliation.
> May the new birth we celebrate
> show its effects in the way we live.
> We ask this through our Lord Jesus Christ, your Son,
> who lives and reigns with you and the Holy Spirit,
> one God, for ever and ever.

EASTER SATURDAY
Mark 16:9–15

M ANY FACTORS MILITATE against belief in our times: a spirit of secularism, a pluralism of belief systems, a moral relativism that refuses to accept any absolute value. Faith is an endangered species. But faith has always been so. Even after being told by Mary Magdalene and the other disciples that the Lord was alive, the apostles continued in their disbelief and stubbornness of heart. The proclamation of the good news would, throughout the generations, fall on deaf ears and skeptical hearts. But then there were always some who believed and cried out glory and praise to God, a cry and proclamation that would echo to the ends of the earth.

Refrain: When Jesus had risen from the dead on the morning after the sabbath, he appeared first to Mary Magdalene, from whom he had cast out seven devils, alleluia.

PIED BEAUTY

Glory be to God for dappled things —
  For skies of couple-colour as a brinded cow;
    For rose-moles all in stipple upon trout that swim;

Fresh-firecoal chestnut-falls; finches' wings;
  Landscapes plotted and pieced — fold, fallow, and plough;
  And all trades, their gear and tackle and trim.

All things counter, original, spare, strange;
  Whatever is fickle, freckled (who knows how?)
  With swift, slow; sweet, sour; adazzle, dim;
He fathers-forth whose beauty is past change:
    Praise him.

Gerard Manley Hopkins

One can only imagine what songs of glory and praise a person would sing when freed from seven demons. Mary Magdalene knew the sickness of sin and the yoke of oppression. She experienced that songless life of little or no self-worth and felt the horror of self-disdain. Then Jesus set her free and taught her the mystery of life, the mystery of her own dignity. Long before she encountered the risen Lord she already knew the mystery of resurrection by way of personal experience. She who was dead was now alive.

If a poet can so eloquently praise and glorify God for the works of creation — skies and rose-moles, finches' wings and landscapes — all things in their marvelous pluralism, how much more can any believer glorify and praise God for the work of salvation. God has set us all free. Sin has been conquered by grace. Darkness gives way to light. Praise him!

Singing is not enough. Worship that is whole overflows into a life of discipleship, a life of service by which we glorify God by living our lives to their full potential. The apostles should have been able to say, after hearing Mary's testimony and that of the other two disciples, praise him! Instead, their vision was so blurred that they sat in the silence and paralysis of unbelief. Jesus entered their dispositions of slowness, sourness, and dimness and transformed them into swift, sweet, adazzle agents of the kingdom. For this we cry out: Praise him!

- *When do you see the glory of God?*

- *Why should worship lead to discipleship?*

- *Does the prayer of praise get as much attention as prayers of petition?*

Praying with the Church

> Father of love,
> by the outpouring of your grace
> you increase the number of those who believe in you.
> Watch over your chosen family.
> Give undying life to all
> who have been born again in baptism.
> Grant this through our Lord Jesus Christ, your Son,
> who lives and reigns with you and the Holy Spirit,
> one God, for ever and ever.

EASTER SEASON
Week Two

SECOND SUNDAY of EASTER
John 20:19–31

S OME INDIVIDUALS cannot accept second-hand knowledge. Without some kind of personal experience, they continue to doubt. Thomas seems to be such a personality type. Words of his fellow disciples were not sufficient to remove his doubt. He had to touch and see for himself. It would be interesting to read "A Gospel according to Thomas" to see how he would approach people like himself who found words and testimony of others insufficient.

Refrain: With your hand, touch the mark of the nails; doubt no longer, but believe, alleluia.

THE ECLIPSE

We could not see the wonder, cloud obscured,
Yet we believed — we knew — it was taking place.
By word of other men we were assured.

Thy word, O God, through ages has endured;
Thy owner doth hold the sun and moon in space;
Yet men doubt Thee, because Thou has veiled Thy face.

Ruth Mary Fox

Concealment causes anxiety in the human heart. We long for certitude, and when things are veiled, be it the affection of a parent, the approval of our peers, our own sense of truth, we experience a darkness that can cause great restlessness and even terror. We were made for light, not darkness.

Revelation happens in various ways. For Thomas it was a primary revelation as the Lord showed his doubting disciples his wounds. For us that revelation is mediated through scripture, through liturgy, through the assuring words of our believing teachers. Faith is demanded when the eclipse takes away our vision of the sun and moon.

God's word endures down through the ages. We are a people of the altar and of the book. The Bible gives us a sense of identity and destiny; God's word opens to us the mystery of creation and redemption; the scriptures direct us unto the path of peace. Though we cannot see God's wonders with the eye of reason, we can see God's gracious mysteries with the eye of faith. In believing in the risen Lord the eclipse will quickly pass.

- *What role does scripture play in your life as a revelation of God?*

- *What wonders of God have you seen during Easter week?*

- *Why is God's face veiled from us?*

Praying with the Church

> Heavenly Father and God of mercy,
> we no longer look for Jesus among the dead,
> for he is alive and has become the Lord of life.
> From the waters of death you raise us with him
> and renew your gift of life within us.
> Increase in our minds and hearts
> the risen life we share with Christ
> and help us to grow as your people
> toward the fullness of eternal life with you.
> We ask this through Christ our Lord.

MONDAY of the SECOND WEEK of EASTER
John 3:1–8

THERE IS NO EVIDENCE that Nicodemus was a poet. Yes, a Pharisee, one knowledgeable about the law and the prosaic side of life, but there is nothing to indicate that his felt feelings and thoughts ever found expression in lyrics. But after encountering Jesus in the darkness of night and being informed of a new birth in water and the Spirit, could it be that this Pharisee's soul was awakened and filled with delight in the loveliness of things, the loveliness of God's Spirit blowing where it will?

Refrain: Truly I tell you, unless you are born again you cannot see the kingdom of God, alleluia.

You Wake My Soul

You wake my soul to fullness of delight
And make more lovely every lovely thing:
The iridescence of the blackbird's wing,
Frail drifting butterflies of gold and white,
Lone shadowy elms in a harvest field at night,
And virgin snows to the cold moon whispering;
All the dear flowers of autumn and of spring,
Through you, have grown more fragrant and more bright.

Always I was aware of loveliness —
But vaguely, as we know when half asleep
Loved voices and faint perfumes or the press
Of a dear hand we grasp and strive to keep —
Until singing into my life you stole
And wakened all the poetry of my soul.

Ruth Mary Fox

In the presence of friends wine does taste sweeter, the moon
appears much clearer, and meadows take on a beauty never before
dreamed of. Friendship brings a spirit of sharing and newness that colors every experience. Through our friendship with
God (which St. Thomas Aquinas calls charity), we are reborn
and are given new eyes to see blackbirds and butterflies and
virgin snow.

Until the Spirit of the risen Lord enters and transforms our
lives we tend not to be all that present to reality. Voices go un-
heeded; perfumes pass us by unnoticed; even a dear hand is hardly
felt because of our anxieties and fears. But once begotten of God
and empowered by the unpredictable Spirit, we become intensely

aware of the loveliness of things, including our own being. We have no need to again ask questions in the night.

Poetry is song. Some say that a poem is a song for people who cannot sing. God's Spirit awakens the poetry in our souls and invites us to proclaim boldly the love of our God. Hopefully it is the type of poetry that leads to justice and peace. Jesus broke Nicodemus out of his literalness in describing another type of rebirth than that of going back into a mother's womb. Jesus sang the poetry of God which brings about rebirth anytime, anywhere. The risen Lord is still with us to awaken our soul.

- *What questions do you ask God in the night? in the daylight?*

- *What is the date of your birth and what is the date of your rebirth?*

- *What rating do you give your soul in terms of "wakened"?*

Praying with the Church

> Almighty and ever-living God,
> your Spirit made us your children,
> confident to call you Father.
> Increase your Spirit of love within us
> and bring us to our promised inheritance.
> Grant this through our Lord Jesus Christ, your Son,
> who lives and reigns with you and the Holy Spirit,
> one God, for ever and ever.

TUESDAY of the SECOND WEEK of EASTER
John 3:7b–15

NICODEMUS WAS A TEACHER and should have known what was the essence of religion and the spiritual life. When Jesus spoke to him about the Spirit and heavenly things, Nicodemus drew a blank. Our Lord then exercised his authority as teacher and spoke directly of what mattered the most: eternal life. And as we know from other biblical passages, the essence of eternal life has to do with love. Jesus came to testify and witness to this love by his total self-giving.

Refrain: I am the Alpha and the Omega, the first and the last, the beginning and the end; I am the root and offspring of David's race; I am the splendor of the morning star, alleluia.

My Prayer

Teach me to love you truly, O my God;
    Earnestly I implore,
And may the sole return for all my love
    Be grace
To love you more.

Ruth Mary Fox

What do you ask of the Lord? To implore God for good health, for economic security, for political freedom, for educational opportunities, for peace in the world are valid expressions of faith. But there is one thing that is truly necessary (that *unum necessarium*), namely, love. Again and again we come to Jesus our guide and savior and ask to be taught how to love, how to give ourselves to others as he did. To be ignorant of love is to be ignorant of our humanity.

And if we truly love others and God with our whole mind and heart and soul, what then might we ask for? The moon? Heaven? The poet suggests that we pray simply to be given more grace so that we might even more generously love God and others. Having broken out of that suffocating life of selfishness, we find ourselves in a happy circle of love. It is this love that leads to eternal life, that scatters the darkness of ignorance, that truly indicates where the Spirit blows.

During this Easter season we are invited to enter more deeply into the mind and heart of Jesus so that we might see our everyday experiences in the light of eternity.

Jesus came down to us so that we might rise up with him to the fullness of life. By participating in his life, suffering, death, and resurrection we come to know experientially the love of God. Our response must be one of being a glad instrument of this love in a rather dark and fragile world.

- *What do you ask for in prayer?*

- *How has God taught you about the mystery of life?*

- *Are there any signs to measure the quality of our love? Markings such as respect, caring, giving?*

Praying with the Church

All powerful God,
help us to proclaim the power of the Lord's resurrection.

May we who accept this sign of the love of Christ
come to share the eternal life he reveals,
for he lives and reigns with you and the Holy Spirit,
one God, for ever and ever.

WEDNESDAY of the SECOND WEEK of EASTER
John 3:16–21

GOD'S GIFTS ARE MANY, but none more significant than divine self-giving in Jesus. "God loved the world so much that he gave us his son...." Of course, the embracing of this gift demands another: the gift of faith. It is through this virtue that we welcome Jesus into our hearts, rely on his amazing grace, submit our wills to his, and give joyful and faithful assent to his word. In so doing we live in the light and have no fear. There is only one response in the end: "Thanks be to God" — *"Deo gratias."*

Refrain: God loved the world so much that he gave his only Son to save all who have faith in him, and to give them eternal life, alleluia.

DEO GRATIAS

I thank You, Lord, for all that You have given:
I thank You for the mountains and the sea,
For this fair earth and Your much fairer heaven
Which holds Your promises for eternity.

I thank You for Your lesser gifts. Oh Lord,
    Your special gifts to me — my home, my friends —
For the health of mind and body these afford!
    I count each gift Your tender goodness sends.

But most of all I wish to thank You, God,
    For Your best gifts — for grief and bitter loss,
For hours of pain beneath Your chastening rod,
    For grace to stand alone beneath Your cross.

For what You have given and what You have denied
    I thank you, Lord, at this Thanksgiving tide.

Ruth Mary Fox

Whether we are in the Easter season or Thanksgiving time, whether we are in weather clement or inclement, whether our days are filled with success or failure, the mature disciple has learned to say that it is good to give thanks to the Lord. The blessings are so many: mountains that remind us of our true size; seas that speak of the vastness of divinity; family and friends who incarnate God's love and mercy; physical and mental health that enable us to live full lives. Such tender goodness is overwhelming and elicits abundant thanks.

But there are other, darker, better "gifts." At least this poet thinks so. How is it possible to express gratitude to God for the grief of a loved one or the loss of sight and hearing? How is it possible to say that God is good, much less give God thanks, when we walk the corridors of our nursing homes or see the tragic documentaries on war or taste our own diminishment? Is this not some neurotic form of sadism, unworthy to be given a religious interpretation? Yet the poet is persistent and sees these griefs and losses as a participation in the cross. And to be in that difficult but privileged place is a great grace.

To give thanks in time of adversity tests the temper of our discipleship. Perhaps it is only looking back that we whisper our *"Deo Gratias."* Much faith and grace is needed if we are to bless God not only in times of abundance but also in times of denial. If thanksgiving is not forthcoming, we yield to resentment and bitterness. We must live with the conviction that whatever God sends us or allows to happen in our lives, in some way, can and will lead to a sharing in his perpetual love.

- *What gifts did God give you during this past Lenten season? And your response?*

- *How do you give explicit expression of thanksgiving to God?*

- *How do you deal with grief and bitter loss?*

Praying with the Church

> God of mercy,
> you have filled us with the hope of resurrection
> by restoring us to our original dignity.
> May we who relive this mystery each year
> come to share it in perpetual love.
> Grant this through our Lord Jesus Christ, your Son,
> who lives and reigns with you and the Holy Spirit,
> one God, for ever and ever.

THURSDAY of the SECOND WEEK of EASTER
John 3:31–36

HAVING COME FROM GOD, Jesus walked the earth. What he had seen and heard in the Father's presence must have given his voice a certain quality, his eyes a certain light. Did he feel an exile in time, having experienced eternity? How could he so graciously embrace the severe limitations of the human condition? Only love could do such a thing. Only divine love made manifest in Jesus could have borne all the responsibility entrusted to him. Jesus was sent by the Father in the fullness of the Spirit to give us eternal life. He came from that undiscovered country to bring us home.

Refrain: The Father loves the Son and has entrusted everything to him, alleluia.

SOME DID RETURN

The undiscovered country from whose bourne
No traveler returns.
Hamlet iii, Scene i, 79–80

Ah, but some did return: the widow's son
The girl Jairus loved, and he for whom
Martha and Mary wept! These Jesus won
Back to mortality, snatched from the tomb.
They did come back. But they have left no word
Of that far country to which we must go
Who never will return. What they have seen and heard
Until we reach that bourne we shall not know.

There must have been a strange light in the eyes
Lit by a soul that had seen heaven and God.
For one who had passed the judgment, great surprise
At things that men call good. He must have trod
The earth an alien. Silent he must be
For want of words who has glimpsed eternity.

Ruth Mary Fox

It is difficult to speak adequately of earthly things. Just try in twenty-five words or less to define justice, or describe a rainbow, or tell of your first love. How much more difficult to speak of a glimpse of eternity. Even the people who have had near death experiences are left to a fragmented stammering.

To bear witness means to tell what happened, what we have seen and heard. Jesus testified to the truthfulness of God giving us the option of receiving or rejecting his revelation. So we hear about the father of the prodigal son, we see Jesus at Cana performing his first miracle of compassion. We stand at the Jordan and hear what happens as Jesus is baptized. But we have no words from the widow's son, Jairus's daughter, the brother of Martha and Mary. Only silence about what lies beyond the edge of time.

We can only wonder what that far country is like. Our notion of goodness is so inadequate compared to God's vision; our concept of holiness, so limited in the presence of divine love; our desires and hope, far too small to encompass God's extravagant gift of eternal life. Perhaps there is a hidden blessing in our ignorance of things to come, for should we know too much, our time on earth might be too alien and our yearning for home too much for our finite hearts to bear.

- *Have you had any glimpses of eternity?*

- *Have you met persons who have the light of holiness in their eyes?*

- *When do you witness to others of the things of God?*

Praying with the Church

> God of mercy,
> may the Easter mystery we celebrate
> be effective throughout our lives.
> Grant this through our Lord Jesus Christ, your Son,
> who lives and reigns with you and the Holy Spirit,
> one God, for ever and ever.

FRIDAY of the SECOND WEEK of EASTER
John 6:1–15

GOD ENCOUNTERS US in various ways. We meet God in the mystery of creation, in the historical moments of birth and death, in the words of scared scripture, in the person of Jesus Christ. The people on the Galilean hillside met God through the breaking of bread and the teachings of Jesus. As these people were fed body and soul they knew themselves to be the object of divine concern. One wonders how many of the five thousand went home that night and, as they traveled, brought to others the good news they heard and the love they experienced.

Refrain: Jesus took bread, and when he had given thanks, he gave it to those who were at table with him, alleluia.

CARRYING CHRIST

Into the hillside country Mary went
Carrying Christ, and all along the road
The Christ she carried generously bestowed
His grace on those she met. She had not meant
To tell she carried Christ. She was content
To hide His love for her. But about her glowed
Such joy that into stony hearts love flowed,
And even to the unborn John Christ's grace was sent.

Christ in His Sacrament of love each day
Dwells in my soul a little space and then
I walk life's crowded highway, jostling men
Who seldom think of God. To these I pray
That I may carry Christ, for it may be
Some would not know of Him except through me.

Ruth Mary Fox

Mary carried Jesus in her womb and in her heart. As she journeyed to see her cousin Elizabeth, when she went to the well to draw water for the family, when she swept the floor or kneaded the bread, Christ was within her accompanying her every step of the way. Though that presence was not visible to the human eye, what could be seen was the radiance of joy that touched all who encountered her.

We carry Christ because of our baptism, confirmation, and reception of the Eucharist. Jesus continues to break open his word and his life to all who have faith. Like Mary, a divine guest has taken up residence in our hearts and we never travel alone. When we are conscious of this presence and become increasingly aware of this treasure of grace, a joy erupts within our hearts so that even strangers might question the source of their radiance and glory.

Each of us walks "life's crowded highway." It could well be that the people we encounter have not yet encountered Jesus, have not yet heard or seen the good news of salvation, have not yet been evangelized. It could well be that we are God's agent to make present to this person, this meeting, this wake service the very presence of Christ. What a noble mission, what a serious responsibility, what a happy calling.

- *Who are the people who have carried Christ to you?*

- *How can you strengthen your devotion to the Eucharist during this Easter season?*

- *Whom can you carry Christ to this very day?*

Praying with the Church

> Father,
> in your plan of salvation
> your Son Jesus Christ accepted the cross
> and freed us from the power of the enemy.
> May we come to share the glory of his resurrection,
> for he lives and reigns with you and the Holy Spirit,
> one God, for ever and ever.

SATURDAY of the SECOND WEEK of EASTER
John 6:16–21

T HE EASTER SEASON speaks so powerfully and insistently of the risen life. But always we are aware of the mystery of death that still surrounds us. It takes but a storm at sea, a tornado on land, a doctor's report of a serious illness to stir up the fear and terror of death. The night is dark and the winds of human vulnerability so strong. Honesty demands that we admit our fear, but faith invites us to trust that Jesus walks toward us at every juncture of life. We are not alone now nor will we be at the hour of our death.

Refrain: Peace be with you; it is I, alleluia; do not be afraid, alleluia.

VIATICUM

Oh my Beloved! How well you know the way
Across infinity which I must go
When on my numbing senses falls the slow
Command, "Depart, O soul, this your day."
Each morning awestruck I watch you obey
The humblest priest as first You sped below
Instant as Mary's Fiat, and I know
The mystery that You both come and stay.

You know the way? You are the Way! O come
To be the Way with me in Your great love,
To go the way with me twixt here and home;
And like a child, calm, trustful, I shall move
Into the dark held close in Your embrace
Nor fear the blinding beauty of Your face.

Ruth Mary Fox

Jesus is the way, the truth, and the life. Our Christian lives are grounded in the radical conviction of God's abiding, loving presence. This faith is tested especially when death approaches and our body begins to diminish. Does God really care? Is Christ really present? Will the Spirit strengthen us in the darkness that surrounds the mystery of death? We pray for the gift of trust that enables us to say yes in the midst of fear.

Jesus traveled the darkness and has blazed the path through dusky woods. Our Lord knew those final days of torture and death. We can identify with his asking that the cup not be given, with the cry of abandonment on the cross. Yet he held firm in faith and uttered his yes to the Father. He does know the way for he walked it. We need but join him and travel together toward our final destiny.

Beauty, it would seem, should not be an object of fear. Yet the blinding beauty of God's love and mercy is too much for our finite souls to comprehend and experience. Like the disciples in the midnight storm they trembled when the blinding glory of Jesus' presence appeared to them. But then how quickly they were home, on shore, away from the terror of the sea.

- *Why is the denial of death such a part of our culture?*

- *What is your level of trust in the face of life's problems?*

- *Is Jesus "the Way" for you or do you travel another path?*

Praying with the Church

> God our Father,
> look upon us with love.
> You redeem us and make us your children in Christ.
> Give us true freedom
> and bring us to the inheritance you promised.
> We ask this through our Lord Jesus Christ, your Son,
> who lives and reigns with you and the Holy Spirit,
> one God, for ever and ever.

Week Three

THIRD SUNDAY of EASTER
Luke 24:13–35 (A); Luke 24:35–48 (B); John 21:1–19 (C)

J ESUS HAD MANY MEALS with his disciples and friends. When invited by strangers and "sinners" Jesus said yes and sat at their tables. In the sharing of food and drink, in the sharing of words and ideas, lives came together and destinies were shaped. The risen Lord continued to encounter his friends in the breaking of the bread, in the cooking of fish, in early morning breakfasts. The Lord has left us the Eucharist so that we might continue to hear his voice and taste his love. Hopefully the gift of the Eucharistic meal will lead us to share our food and lives with others.

Refrain: It was ordained that Christ should suffer, and on the third day rise from the dead, alleluia.

FOUR THOUSAND SUPPERS

At the kitchen table
at six o'clock.
Dark winter evenings
with my father in his
winter underwear,

quilted like an astronaut.
Blue summer evenings
after my mother called my name
on the lilting breeze
which reached me
at far corners
of the neighborhood,
her voice known
among all the others.

We ate
four thousand suppers
in that small room together.
What did we discuss?
Linoleum and carpet,
casement windows,
the wild McElroys,
the loud Mrs. Supportas,
scenes from the fifth grade,
my problems with bushels and pecks.
Four thousand suppers —
oceans of tea.
The man and woman
at the table
grow grey.
I grow up —
feet finally
reach the floor.

Anne Higgins

We all sat at our own kitchen table, year after year, season after season. Our memories tell of conversations and arguments, of food fit for a king or queen and meals hurriedly put together, of laughter and tears. For some of us, those breakfasts, lunches, suppers, and dinners were events of extreme joy and happiness; for others, perhaps, meals were occasions of silence and tension because of strained relationships and a lack of love.

All are invited to another table, the table of the Lord. It is here that we hear conversation that tells of God's love and mercy, of promises of eternal life and forgiveness of sin, of the importance of love and kindness in a broken world. At this table we encounter the living Christ who once again gives us himself so that we might have the strength and courage to be servants of the good news and stewards of creation. At the table we are fed with the bread of life and sent forth to share our gifts with others.

Maybe after ten or thirty or sixty years of coming to the Eucharist, our feet might finally touch the floor. Maturity is a long process, as long as conversion. In baptism we are called to holiness and service, to community and maturity. Those calls need the grace of Eucharist to be heard and responded to. Perhaps after four thousand suppers we will come to the point that dying to ourselves — tasting the paschal mystery — will become a way of life.

- *At what age did your feet touch the floor of maturity?*

- *What did you talk about at your kitchen table as a child? Today?*

- *Whom do you invite over for supper?*

Praying with the Church

> Father in heaven, author of all truth,
> a people once in darkness have listened to your Word
> and followed your Son as he rose from the tomb.
> Hear the prayer of this newborn people
> and strengthen your Church to answer your call.
> May we rise and come forth into the light of day
> to stand in your presence until eternity dawns.
> We ask this through Christ our Lord. Amen.

MONDAY of the THIRD WEEK of EASTER
John 6:22–29

SEARCHING IS A MAJOR ACTIVITY on this human journey. We search for security, for prestige, for knowledge and love, for that "something" that will end all longings. Most often our hunt involves some type of "perishable food" — more money, a bigger house, a higher rung on the academic or corporate ladder. Jesus instructs us that there is an eternal longing that can be satisfied only by faith. In the end, it is not so much our search for God as it is God's search for us as he sends Jesus across to the lake to remind us what the works of God truly are.

Refrain: Do not work for food that will perish, but for food that lasts to eternal life, alleluia.

Sitz im Leben

Who sits in my life,
makes me rise like water
around him?
Who contains me
like wine in a bottle,
who dwells within
like light in a candle?
Athens backs away from him.
Corinth opens her arms.
His words make me
His arrow, hiding,
His hand, gloved.

Anne Higgins

Water is a symbol of life. God's work in baptism washes us clean and plunges us into the life of grace. Our rebirth in the baptismal font means that the life of Christ permeates our entire existence. We sit in the ocean of God's love and mercy. Prayer is a time in which we become aware of this immersion; it provides the opportunity to know experientially the rising of this water within our souls.

Wine is a symbol of joy and companionship. But the joy is not so much in the drink itself as in the company of those with whom we share it and thereby share our lives. The psalmist tells us that God delights in us. We are God's precious wine and are God's possession. We are given, as was Jesus, as food and drink for others that they may have life to the full. Hopefully we are good wine, well aged, and delightful to the taste.

Candles are not just symbols of light but actually produce

warmth. One of the works of God is that of indwelling. The Spirit has been given to us; we are temples of that Spirit. A light burns bright within and we strive for a transparency so that through our lives others may see. If so, people will not back away from the message of Christ coming through our lives, but will open their arms to the person of Christ and open their minds to hear his saving words.

- *Which metaphor — water, wine, candle — speaks most clearly to you of God's indwelling presence?*

- *Who are the people in your life who bring you God's word?*

- *How can we become God's arrow and hand in the world today?*

Praying with the Church

God our Father,
your light of truth
guides us to the way of Christ.
May all who follow him
reject what is contrary to the Gospel.
We ask this through our Lord Jesus Christ, your Son,
who lives and reigns with you and the Holy Spirit,
one God, for ever and ever.

TUESDAY of the THIRD WEEK of EASTER
John 6:30–35

I N ALFRED, LORD TENNYSON'S POEM "Ulysses" we read: "He works his work, I mine." Not so with Jesus. The work that Jesus came to do is the same work as the Father. The work that disciples are entrusted to do is the same work as that of Jesus. Ultimately it was not Moses who gave people bread from heaven; it is not our parents who give us life; it is not our teachers who ground us in truth. Rather, all life and truth and holiness come from God, and it is God alone who can satisfy our hunger and thirst. It is at the altar that we find our meaning and nourishment.

Refrain: Truly I say to you: Moses did not give you the bread of heaven; my Father gives you the true bread from heaven, alleluia.

THE VILLA MASS

The old sisters
sing at the Offertory:
Heart of Jesus, meek and mild,
in two part harmony,
words the world
stopped singing before we were born.
Blue veins,
twig fingers,
voices like new bells
call Jesus.

His children,
their voices
in the air

project old films:
limber legs
rushing to school,
wool, starch,
waxing the floors by hand,
rising at four,
white linen,
long sickness
like grim guests
waiting in the parlor.
Their armies
have gone
to a handful.
Now, we kneel
behind them,
help them to the altar
where we are
their only rail.

Anne Higgins

God's work of creation and redemption and sanctification becomes ours through baptism. Though the work is essentially the
same, the work of love and service, it does take on different
forms. We have "our" work to do in tending the land as farm-
ers, in healing the sick as nurses, in raising a family as dads and
moms, in instructing and guiding the young as teachers, in wit-
nessing to the Gospel through vows of obedience, poverty, and
chastity as religious.

But all of us bring our gifts to the altar. We come to the Lord,
meek and mild, courageous and strong. We sing our hymns of

praise and petition in deep faith, knowing that God will nourish our minds with meaningful words and tend our souls through the gift of the Eucharist. And we bring to the altar our entire lives, our energetic youth and morning sacrifices, our weaknesses and sins, our days of health and sickness. And God takes us just as we are.

As a community we have a special duty toward the elderly and frail. We stand behind them in support and we gaze upon them in admiration. They are the ones who have fought the fight and so often at great personal cost. They are the ones who might wonder if it was all worthwhile. Our presence behind and beside them is assurance that nothing is lost and that God's work will continue.

- *What specific work has God given you to do?*

- *Who are the people whom you support in their latter years?*

- *What meaning does the Mass hold for you?*

Praying with the Church

> Father,
> you open the kingdom of heaven
> to those born again by water and the Spirit.
> Increase your gift of love in us.
> May all who have been freed from sins in baptism
> receive all that you have promised.
> We ask this through our Lord Jesus Christ, your Son,
> who lives and reigns with you and the Holy Spirit,
> one God, for ever and ever.

WEDNESDAY of the THIRD WEEK of EASTER
John 6:35–40

GOD HAS DRAFTED a magnificent blueprint. It is one not concerned with flying buttresses or Roman arches, not with stained-glass windows and golden altars but rather with the person of his Son who will do his will. The blueprint for salvation will be lived love, a love and obedience unto death. The plan will involve a dying and a rising, a letting go that all might be gained. God's architectural plans are filled with paradoxes and drifting shadows, with sunbeams and the ability to say yes.

Refrain: Whoever sees the Son and believes in him will live forever, and I shall raise him up on the last day, alleluia.

DRAFTING SHADOWS

When the architect
planned the church,
did he ever stand on
the bare ground
at nine on a sunny morning
in February,
and see where his shadow fell?
Did he envision that sun
tilting through the windows,
high windows,
hitting the huge cross
so that its shadow
struck the far wall
just as people were saying,

"He has come to his people
and set us free."

Could he in his mind
measure how high
to place those windows
with some geometry
of the imagination,
up in the invisible wall
below an invisible dome,
placing an hypotenuse
of sunbeam
into the mosaic of
an enormous eye?

Anne Higgins

The design of any church must have a focus. Where will the sunlight fall? As the cross is illuminated, we come to know that we have been set free through this ultimate sacrifice. Jesus, though trembling in the garden, did the will of his Father and through the incarnation and redemption liberated us so that we are now free from sin and can worship the Lord without fear. Were the sun not to fall on the cross, our churches, in spite of artificial lighting, would be dark places.

God and architects have keen imaginations. They can see what is not yet there: walls, domes, peace, the kingdom. It is the imagination of faith that enables us to picture the kingdom, the rule of God in our hearts and our communities. In the end our churches are not structures of dead stones but are living people, and it is we who are called to be transparent to God's grace. Through us the light must shine and illumine a dark world. God's architectural design can be better seen in a humble gathering of believers in prayer than in the majesty of Notre Dame Cathedral in Paris.

And yet our church buildings are so important, as is our music and liturgy. God comes to us sacramentally, and so the angle of light, the smell of incense, the haunting mosaic, the meaningful crucifix can all mediate the mysteries of our belief. We should all pray that architects experience their February shadows, that all musicians understand the geometry of the imagination, that all liturgists understand the hypotenuse of the cross.

- *Where does the angle of the sun fall in the church where you celebrate?*

- *If you were to design a church, what would it look like?*

- *What sacramentals foster your belief? The cross? Stained-glass windows? The rosary?*

Praying with the Church

> Merciful Lord,
> hear the prayers of your people.
> May we who have received your gift of faith
> share forever in the new life of Christ.
> Grant this through our Lord Jesus Christ, your Son,
> who lives and reigns with you and the Holy Spirit,
> one God, for ever and ever.

THURSDAY of the THIRD WEEK of EASTER
John 6:44–51

I T WAS THE POET GOETHE who once wrote that "not to know this, to die and so to rise, is to always be a troubled guest on the dark earth." Jesus invites us into his paschal meal, into his dying and rising, so that we might be good stewards on this long pilgrimage. Our lives are not essentially about a process (even the process of dying/rising) but rather about a person, about putting on the mind and heart of our Lord. It is the Father who draws us and instructs us as to the mystery of Jesus. Our belief in him leads to eternal life beyond death and a meaningful life here on earth.

Refrain: Amen, amen, I say to you: Whoever believes in me will live forever, alleluia.

RECIPE

Yeast rises
like praise
clings to the cloth,
leavens its thready face there.

Dough rolls smooth
springs back
seamless in hand
as thought.

The oven opens and closes
its arms.
Smell seeps
from room to room.

Bread, as finished
as a child.
Every slice of the knife
it sings its fearful litany:
I live in the jaws of hunger.
I break as I give
I rise as I die.

Anne Higgins

For some of us the aroma of home-made bread brings back pleasant memories of childhood. Even the theft of raw dough (a minor felony) gave a foretaste of a delicious meal to come. Watching the miracle of dough rising filled us with wonder. At the evening meal, a warm piece of bread covered with gravy or smothered with butter was an early experience of the kingdom.

We all live in the "jaws of hunger." Home-made bread satiates the stomach for a few hours, but too soon the gnawing returns. Our longings focus on another bread from another land. Our souls yearn for belonging and meaning, for depth and wholeness. But it is strange that unless the bread is broken or sliced, it cannot be shared and give life.

So we are back, always back, to the person of Jesus and to his invitation to die in order to rise. We are broken as we are given, and we die as we rise. Could the grain of wheat know this, it would sing songs of praise at the harvest, and the acorn would sing songs of thanksgiving as it falls from the oak tree. We who should be in the know are frequently the ones ignorant of this paschal mystery. Unless we have faith, unless the Father draws us into the heart of Christ, we are troubled guests on a dark planet.

- *When was the last time you were in a home when bread was baking?*

- *Are you a good guest on this planet or one with many worries and fears?*

- *What is your history of "breakings" so as to be given, of your "risings" as you die?*

Praying with the Church

> Father, in this holy season
> we come to know the full depth of your love.
> You have freed us from the darkness of error and sin.
> Help us to cling to your truths with fidelity.
> We ask this through our Lord Jesus Christ, your Son,
> who lives and reigns with you and the Holy Spirit,
> one God, for ever and ever.

FRIDAY of the THIRD WEEK of EASTER
John 6:52–59

THE EUCHARIST is God's stained-glass window. Here we have the story of infinite love taking on finite form in the simple elements of bread and wine. This is not mere symbolism and metaphor. Here we have real food, real drink, in the gift of Jesus to humankind. During the Easter season we do well to stand before this window and drink in its meaning and beauty. Better yet, during this season we continue to taste the real presence of Jesus in word and sacrament. By so doing we shall live forever even as our cathedrals crumble and our symbols give way to the fullness of reality.

Refrain: Whoever eats my flesh and drinks my blood shall live in me and I in him, alleluia.

THE SPACE WINDOW AT THE WASHINGTON CATHEDRAL

In the midst of Gothic
pointing, stretching,
stone and smell of spring
window stories
of God
coming to earth,
is a breath-catching
view of earth
coming to God.
Here is a glimpse, outside
our field
into deep of swirling
pinwheel planets and stars
in a Van Gogh, Hopkins
himmel hock
and hosanna in excelsis
shining on us
in a bath of purple
Revelation,
unframed,
unstoned.

Anne Higgins

The great cathedrals of the world are storytellers. For those who have eyes to see, these massive structures reveal the relationship between God and humankind. At times the stories will originate in the heart of God as we see in the garden of Eden and the crucifixion of Jesus. At other times the stories are told from the human point of view, our striving toward transcendence at the burning bush and in the tempests on Lake Galilee.

All the stories are about life and death, joys and sorrows, trust and anguish. The windows depict the planets and the stars as well as the manger and the cross. We witness Moses on Mount Sinai and Peter before the evening fire. We are given a glimpse of creation as God cries out, "And it was good," as well as a picture of human cruelty as innocent children are slain around Bethlehem.

Our modern cathedrals attempt to portray our contemporary experiences of space. We have here yet another form of revelation, however unframed or unstoned, by which we catch glimpses of our God. There is now a hole in the heavens, and we can see far into the galaxies, a seeing that expands our sense of mystery and awe. Yet we always come back to the window showing the Last Supper. In this framed revelation we find a solid rock upon which to construct a life of faith.

- *What are your favorite pieces of art depicting your faith?*

- *Are there any cathedrals that have enriched your spiritual journey?*

- *If you could list the components of a cathedral window to capture the essentials of the Eucharist, what would those components be?*

Praying with the Church

> Father,
> by the love of your Spirit,
> may we who have experienced
> the grace of the Lord's resurrection
> rise to the newness of life in joy.
> Grant this through our Lord Jesus Christ, your Son,
> who lives and reigns with you and the Holy Spirit,
> one God, for ever and ever.

SATURDAY of the THIRD WEEK of EASTER
John 6:60–69

PETER is one of the most attractive personalities in the scriptures. He is bold, practical, impulsive; he is weak, presumptuous, muddle-headed. The apostle, so loved by the Lord, is usually the first to speak, and his instincts are true. The Lord does have the words of eternal life, and there is no one else worth following. Though he would later deny the Lord at the campfire, he would shed his tears, repent, and become the leader of the faith community. Peter is attractive and beloved because he is so human, so real. His experiences and responses are so much like our own.

Refrain: Simon Peter said: Lord, to whom shall we go? You have the words of eternal life; and we believe and we are convinced that you are the Christ, the Son of God, alleluia.

IN THE PHILLIPS GALLERY: THE REPENTANT PETER

Goya and El Greco
both painted him.
Goya's man looks to the West —
up and forward,
his melon face
bald, practical,
used to laughter.
Strong fat peasant arms
extend out
and clasped to heaven,
keys set aside
on the arm of the sofa.

El Greco saw him
stretched
with a long sad
poet's face,
shadowed cheeks,
eyes drawn down
at the outside corners,
looking East.
His clasped hands pull in
toward his heart;

the keys still
hooked to his belt.

The two of them
have just heard the cock crow.
They face each other
from the walls
of neighboring rooms in the gallery
through a wide doorway.

Anne Higgins

Artists paint their personal perspective and we viewers see from our own angle. We have the light-hearted Peter and can hear his strong voice and boisterous laughter. Then we have the Peter whose heart is fragmented after betrayal and whose cheeks are tear-stained. So much of life depends upon our moral decisions, our making and keeping promises, our relationships.

When the cock crows the truth is out. The early conviction of faith fails in the face of temptation. The fear is so great that Peter cannot withstand the pressure and denies that he knows Jesus, the very one who has the words of eternal life. None of us can enter judgment here, for all of us have moments and seasons of denial and betrayal as well. We all stand in need of God's mercy. Our faith is so easily shaken.

When all is said and done God is faithful. Peter still retains the keys and is commissioned to go out and proclaim the good news of God's love and mercy in Jesus. Though a sense of unworthiness must have pursued him all the days of his life, Peter assumed the responsibility of sharing the words of eternal life with all those he ministered to.

- *What is your highest appraisal of Peter?*

- *What set of keys (set of responsibilities) has the Lord given you?*

- *How does God remind you of your infidelities?*

Praying with the Church

God our Father,
by the waters of baptism
you give new life to the faithful.
May we not succumb to the influence of evil
but remain true to your gift of life.
We ask this through our Lord Jesus Christ, your Son,
who lives and reigns with you and the Holy Spirit,
one God, for ever and ever.

Week Four

FOURTH SUNDAY of EASTER
John 10:1–10 (A); John 10:11–18 (B); John 10:27–30 (C)

T HE MYSTERY OF JESUS is partially disclosed through various concepts and images. Jesus is both human and divine; he is the victim-lamb and the good shepherd. These different expressions give us various angles of seeing the rich life of our Lord. It takes great faith to believe that the Lord is also the lamb, that the savior of the world is nailed to the tree of the cross. Again this Sunday we ponder the mystery of the risen Lord and become increasingly aware that we are called to conform our lives to his. It is well that we ask the question "who made us?" and the further question "what is this Lord of ours like?"

Refrain: I am the shepherd of the sheep; I am the way, the truth, and the life; I know my sheep, and my sheep know me, alleluia.

THE LAMB

Little Lamb, who made thee?
Dost thou know who made thee?
Gave thee life, and bid thee feed
By the stream and o'er the mead;

Gave thee clothing of delight,
Softest clothing, woolly, bright;
Gave thee such a tender voice,
Making all the vales rejoice?
   Little lamb, who made thee?
   Dost thou know who made thee?

   Little lamb, I'll tell thee,
   Little lamb, I'll tell thee:
He is called by thy name,
For he calls Himself a Lamb,
He is meek, and He is mild;
He became a little child.
I a child, and thou a lamb,
We are called by His name.
   Little lamb, God bless thee!
   Little lamb, God bless thee!

William Blake

According to the spiritual writer Gerald Vann, the condition for happiness is a deep sense of our creatureliness. We are creatures, we are made. In asking the question of who is our creator we are forced to recognize that all is gift — everything! The poet William Blake walks through a meadow and asks a lamb who gave it life and food and water, who provided the pastures, the clothing of wool, the voice that cries out "bah"? No reply is forthcoming, so the poet tells the truth as he sees it. Our God made manifest in Jesus came to us as a lamb and assumed that title. This Lord of life is humble, meek, and mild; this Lord of life became a child and was born of Mary. In this simple children's poem we encounter the mystery of a transcendent God who has taken on the human condition and brought about salvation through self-sacrifice.

Now the question "who made thee?" turns into the declarative statement "God bless thee!" The poet Blake is asking God's blessing on both the lamb and the child. It is the deceptive simplicity of this verse, holding mystery upon mystery (creation, incarnation, salvation) that challenges us to be attentive to the meaning of our own existence.

- *What questions do you ask of God and life itself?*

- *What teachings do you share with those who do not know about God?*

- *Is the image of Christ as "lamb" meaningful to you?*

Praying with the Church

> God and Father of our Lord Jesus Christ,
> though your people walk in the valley of darkness,
> no evil should they fear;
> for they follow in faith the call of the shepherd
> whom you have sent for their hope and strength.
> Attune our minds to the sound of his voice,
> lead our steps in the path he has shown,
> that we may know the strength of his outstretched arm
> and enjoy the light of your presence forever.
> We ask this in the name of Jesus the Lord.

MONDAY of the FOURTH WEEK of EASTER
John 10:1–10 or John 10:11–18

T HE IMAGE OF JESUS as shepherd carries many undertones and overtones: fidelity to the sheep, tender knowing of needs, self-sacrifice for the flock's well-being, affection, and love. In this "human form divine" we catch glimpses of the mystery of God as well as hints and clues to what we are called to do and be. All life is relational. We are all responsible in some way for the well-being of one another. Shepherding, an ancient agrarian image, retains its power to stir our hearts and ignite our imaginations. Though no image captures the fullness of the reality, the image of the good shepherd, if tasted fully, draws us deeply into the nature of God.

Refrain: I am the Good Shepherd; I pasture my sheep and I lay down my life for them, alleluia.

THE DIVINE IMAGE

To Mercy, Pity, Peace, and Love
All pray in their distress;
And to these virtues of delight
Return their thankfulness.

For Mercy, Pity, Peace, and Love
Is God, our Father dear,
And Mercy, Pity, Peace, and Love
Is man, His child and care.

For Mercy has a human heart,
Pity a human face,

And Love, the human form divine,
And Peace, the human dress.

Then every man, of every clime,
That prays in his distress,
Prays to the human form divine,
Love, Mercy, Pity, Peace.

And all must love the human form,
In heathen, Turk, or Jew;
Where Mercy, Love, and Pity dwell
There God is dwelling too.

William Blake

In times of distress — be it hurricane or illness, be it loss of integrity or negligence — we realize in a pressing way our dependence upon God. We cry out for mercy, seek the Lord's pity, hunger for peace, yearn for love. And God is gracious in bestowing these blessings upon our parched souls and broken world. Gratitude is our fitting response and, more, sincere praise.

But these virtues are not abstract philosophical terms. We "see" mercy as Jesus intercedes for the woman caught in adultery while exposing her accusers. We "see" pity as Jesus wept for his friend Lazarus and felt the pain of Mary and Martha. We "see" peace as the disciples in the upper room experienced fear evaporating as Jesus greeted them with a smile. We "see" love on the hill of Calvary where the Lord redeemed the world from sin. God has become visible in Jesus, the divine in human form.

Where does God dwell? *Ubi caritas et amor, Deus ibi est!* ("Where charity and love are, there is God!") And we might add, where peace and pity and mercy are present, there too is God.

Each of us, recipients of these blessings so many times, is now commissioned to give human form to these virtues and thereby fulfill our baptismal calling of making Jesus present to the world in our day. By so doing we fulfill our call as shepherds to further the kingdom.

- *Recall a time when you last experienced mercy, pity, peace, and love.*

- *When have you extended these virtues to others?*

- *What is the quality of your thankfulness to Jesus, the good shepherd?*

Praying with the Church

> Father,
> through the obedience of Jesus,
> your servant and your Son,
> you raised a fallen world.
> Free us from sin
> and bring us the joy that lasts forever.
> We ask this through our Lord Jesus Christ, your Son,
> who lives and reigns with you and the Holy Spirit,
> one God, for ever and ever.

TUESDAY of the FOURTH WEEK of EASTER
John 10:22–30

I T IS IN THE TEMPLE AREA, the house of God, that we get an
insight into the person of Jesus. It was there, when he was
only twelve, that he instructed the teachers. In today's reading, it
is in the temple area that we see Jesus being questioned about his
work and what people expect of him. It is in the temple that Jesus
becomes angry when the money-changers turn God's house into
a commercial enterprise. One can sense again a smoldering anger
as Jesus responds: "I did tell you, but you do not believe." Here
we have a holy anger — an expression of frustration — that God's
design is not being followed.

*Refrain: The works that I do in the name of my Father speak on my
behalf, alleluia.*

A POISON TREE

I was angry with my friend;
I told my wrath, my wrath did end.
I was angry with my foe:
I told it not, my wrath did grow.

And I water'd it in fears,
Night & morning with my tears:
And I sunned it with smiles,
And with soft deceitful wiles.

And it grew both day and night.
Till it bore an apple bright.
And my foe beheld it shine,
And he knew that it was mine.

And into my garden stole,
When the night had veiled the pole:
In the morning glad I see;
My foe outstretch'd beneath the tree.

William Blake

Jesus came to bring us eternal life. But there are poisons that can kill the life of grace, not only within us but in others as well. An unjust anger is one such poison which, unaddressed, grows and wreaks its havoc. Refusal to believe is another, even when evidence is provided that indicates that Jesus is doing the work of his Father.

This poem reminds us of the importance of naming and getting in touch with those "spirits" within us that are destructive and can snatch us off the path to eternal life. In our tradition we speak of the deadly sins of pride, anger, lust, envy, gluttony, greed, sloth. Jesus continually challenges us to get in touch with the truth because it will set us free. It is when we refuse to recognize our wrath, our pride, our greed, and their destructive consequences they gain mastery over our lives.

In the garden of Eden there was the tree of knowledge on which hung the fruits of good and evil. We have to make choices in life of what foods and books, movies and relationships we will partake of. Some of them lead toward eternal life; others contain a deadly poison that gradually carry us toward darkness and death. If we listen to the shepherd's voice and respond, we will eat of the good fruit and know the mystery of eternal life.

- *How well do you do in naming your inner "spirits?"*

- *Do you have any poison in your system now?*

- *Which of the capital sins tend to poison your soul?*

Praying with the Church

> Almighty God,
> as we celebrate the resurrection,
> may we share with each other
> the joy the risen Lord has won for us.
> We ask this through our Lord Jesus Christ, your Son,
> who lives and reigns with you and the Holy Spirit,
> one God, for ever and ever.

WEDNESDAY of the FOURTH WEEK of EASTER
John 12:44–50

G OD'S WORD is absolutely clear: it is *the* Word of salvation, not condemnation. Jesus came to bring life though, paradoxically, it would come by means of death. Jesus came to bring light, though often he walked into darkness to bring hope to the lost and despairing. Jesus continues this work of salvation by bringing life and light to all who sit in the shadow of darkness and death. All creation will be reconciled to the Father. Through Jesus the mystery of God's loving smile touches not just the innocent lamb within all of us but even the fierce tiger.

Refrain: I am the light; I have come into the world, that those who believe in me may not remain in darkness, alleluia.

THE TIGER

Tiger! Tiger! burning bright
In the forests of the night,
What immortal hand or eye
Could frame thy fearful symmetry?

In what distant deeps or skies
Burnt the fire of thine eyes?
On what wings dare he aspire?
What the hand dare seize the fire?

And what shoulder, and what art,
Could twist the sinews of thy heart?
And when thy heart began to beat,
What dread hand? and what dread feet?

What the hammer? what the chain?
In what furnace was thy brain?
What the anvil? what dread grasp
Dare its deadly terrors clasp?

When the stars threw down their spears,
And watered heaven with their tears,
Did he smile his work to see?
Did he who made the Lamb make thee?

Tiger! Tiger! burning bright
In the forests of the night,
What immortal hand or eye
Dare frame thy fearful symmetry?

William Blake

Albert Schweitzer, the Nobel Peace Prize winner, once said that a simple smile across an aisle or room could stop a suicide. We all wonder, at one time or another, whether we are the object of love and affirmation. If a human smile can stay a suicide, how much more the smile of God to instill hope and joy in the human heart. And further, does this smile and love of God reach into the dark forces of our lives?

The forest tiger is a thing of mixed beauty. The fire in its eye brings terror to its prey; the strength of its smooth body causes admiration to the poet; the tiger's strong heart and complex brain make us wonder at the awesomeness of its creator. Contrast the ferocious tiger with the meek and mild lamb and one does wonder if God's smile falls equally on both of them.

And our lives? A mixture of virtue and vice, of love and hate, of goodness and evil! We have been created with that marvelous capacity of freedom, a gift that can take us down the road of life or death, darkness or light. If we are aware of God's unconditional love and experience that love in the person of the risen Lord, we will respond to God's smile by doing good to others and using our freedom in loving and just ways.

- *Pay a visit to a zoo and sit with a tiger for an hour.*

- *Is your image of God one that sees God smiling?*

- *Is your image of God large enough to also see God weeping?*

Praying with the Church

God our Father,
life of the faithful,
glory of the humble,

happiness of the just,
hear our prayer.

Fill our emptiness
with the blessing of the Eucharist,
the foretaste of eternal joy.
We ask this through our Lord Jesus Christ, your Son,
who lives and reigns with you and the Holy Spirit,
one God, for ever and ever.

THURSDAY of the FOURTH WEEK of EASTER
John 13:16–20

O NE OF THE GREAT SIGNS of love in the Gospel is the washing of the feet of the disciples. Jesus does the deed first and
then instructs his followers about doing the same. Putting love
into practice is essentially accepting Jesus into our lives. There is
another possibility, i.e., thinking ourselves above the master and
not having to follow the way of the cross. We can even turn from
"the way" that leads to heaven via the road of love and construct
a hell here on earth by leading lives of selfishness. Perhaps a clod
of clay and pebble can instruct us in this matter.

*Refrain: No disciple is greater than his teacher; he should be glad to
become like his master, alleluia.*

THE CLOD AND THE PEBBLE

"Love seeketh not Itself to please,
Nor for itself hath any care,
But for another gives its ease,
And builds a Heaven in Hell's despair."

So sang a little Clod of Clay,
Trodden with the cattle's feet,
But a Pebble of the brook
Warbled out these metres meet:

"Love seeketh only Self to please,
To bind another to its delight;
Joys in another's loss of ease,
And builds a Hell in Heaven's despite."

William Blake

The philosophers and psychologists have a genius for finding words to describe the various kinds of love. There is the love that focuses simply on self (narcissism). Then there is romantic love that involves high sexual energies. Charity is a third type of love in which we are committed to the growth and well-being of others. Finally there is God's love (agape), which is universal, unconditional, infinite.

The clod of clay and the pebble in Blake's poem tell us that love goes basically in one of two directions: toward or away from self. When love expresses care and concern for us by easing pain and suffering, heaven is being constructed. When, however, we seek only our own pleasure and use others for our benefit and even rejoice in another's pain, the end result will be the house of hell.

Jesus broke into our lostness and despair to bring us heaven, the experience of union with God. If we accept him and his way of life, we will be building the kingdom of God. That means washing one another's feet, feeding the hungry, loving one another as he loved us. Herein lies true joy. The other option is a narrow narcissism that throws us even now into the despair of hell.

- *What is your understanding of the mystery of love?*

- *What is your level of acceptance of Jesus in your life?*

- *How do you deal with pride (of the pebble) and humility (of the clod of clay)?*

Praying with the Church

> Father,
> in restoring human nature
> you have given us a greater dignity
> than we had in the beginning.
> Keep us in your love
> and continue to sustain those
> who have received new life in baptism.
> We ask this through our Lord Jesus Christ, your Son,
> who lives and reigns with you and the Holy Spirit,
> one God, for ever and ever.

FRIDAY of the FOURTH WEEK of EASTER
John 14:1–6

J ESUS KNEW THE FEAR, doubt, and distress the disciples felt
as they sought to understand the consequences of separation
from the teacher and master. Like a mother who takes her son
upon her lap or a teacher who gathers the students in a circle for
serious conversation, Jesus speaks words of consolation and truth.
He declares himself to be way, truth, and life. It is through him
that all can come to dwell in God's golden tent. All that is needed
is a childlike faith, believing that the words of one's parent are
worthy of trust.

*Refrain: I go now to prepare a place for you, but I shall return to take
you with me, so that where I am you also may be, alleluia.*

THE LITTLE BLACK BOY

My mother bore me in the southern wild,
And I am black, but O! my soul is white;
White as an angel is the English child,
But I am black, as if bereaved of light.

My mother taught me underneath a tree,
And sitting down before the heat of day,
She took me on her lap and kissed me,
And, pointing to the east, began to say:

"Look on the rising sun — there God does live
And gives His light, and gives His heat away;
And flower and trees and beasts and men receive
Comfort in morning, joy in the noonday.

"And we are put on earth a little space,
That we may learn to bear the beams of love;
And these black bodies and this sunburnt face
Is but a cloud, and like a shady grove.

"For when our souls have learned the heat to bear,
The cloud will vanish; we shall hear His voice,
Saying: 'Come out from the grove, My love and care,
And round My golden tent like lambs rejoice.'"

Thus did my mother say and kissed me;
And thus I say to little English boy.
When I from black and he from white cloud free,
And round the tent of God like lambs we joy,

I'll shade him from the heat, till he can bear
To lean in joy upon our Father's knee;
And then I'll stand and stroke his silver hair,
And be like him, and he will then love me.

William Blake

Too often there are factors that cause us to be separated from
one another and even from God. The color of one's skin, an eth-
nic background, a certain level of intelligence, the lack of power
or wealth, and the list goes on. Beneath all these extrinsic elements we are all God's children and are called to rejoice in God's
single tent, the dwelling we call heaven.

Jesus came to tell us God's tale. We need but look on the rising
sun or reflect on the mystery of creation to learn of God's many
gifts. We need but realize that we are here on earth for one reason: the reception and giving away of love. We need but listen
attentively as God calls everyone to enter his golden tent.

It is all a matter of freedom, freedom from prejudice, from racism, from sin. Our challenge is to love one another as Jesus did, he who is our way, truth, and life. By becoming the community God wants us to be and by sustained caring and compassion we live as God's pilgrim people. Each morning it is wise to sit upon our Savior's lap to hear the retelling of God's loving design.

- *Why were you placed here on this earth?*

- *Do you have to struggle with any deep prejudices that cause a tear in God's seamless garment?*

- *Is there anyone today that you can tell "the story" to, the story of God's creation, redemption, and sanctification in Jesus?*

Praying with the Church

Father of our freedom and salvation,
hear the prayers of those redeemed by your Son's suffering.
Through you may we have life;
with you may we have eternal joy.
We ask this through our Lord Jesus Christ, your Son,
who lives and reigns with you and the Holy Spirit,
one God, for ever and ever.

SATURDAY of the FOURTH WEEK of EASTER
John 14:7–14

HAVE YOU EVER been startled by the question: "How much do you know about God?" Had this question been asked of Philip the disciple of the Lord, we might be astounded by this answer. Philip had spent considerable time in the presence of Jesus and yet did not know much at all, it seems, about the mystery of God. One can sense the frustration in Jesus' voice: "I have been with you all this time...." What about us, we who have a rich tradition of two thousand years, we who have a rich sacramental life, we who have been given so many grains of sand and so many wild flowers? How much do we know about God?

Refrain: When the prince of pastors comes again, you will receive from him an unfolding crown of glory, alleluia.

FROM AUGURIES OF INNOCENCE

To see a World in a Grain of Sand,
And a Heaven in a Wild Flower:
Hold Infinity in the palm of your hand,
And Eternity in an hour.

William Blake

God breaks into our lives by so many avenues. Creation is one of them, and St. Paul reminds us that we have no excuse in not knowing God because the Creator is revealed in creation. Our task is to pay attention: to see the mountains and oceans, to hear the infinite longing of the wind, to feel the force of fire, to gaze intently at burning bushes and flowers in crannied walls.

But the great revelation is the person of Jesus. In our God-made-man we are given the ultimate sign of God's self-disclosing love. Not only did God create (and still creates) the world, but our God through the mystery of the incarnation plunges into it and identifies with our human condition. Our task is to be open to the mind and heart of Jesus and to experience his redemptive love as a personal grace.

Still our knowledge of God can be held in the palm of our hand and God's eternal presence can be experienced in time, in this very hour. It is both a matter of faith here — to believe in the works of God — and a matter of reverence and awe. A grain of sand, a fallen leaf, a summer rainbow have the power to take us out of ourselves (ecstasy) and draw us into the great mystery of a creating God. Never again will time be the same. There will be an eternal component in all hours and minutes because we know that the giver of time waits to encounter us at every moment.

- *When was the last time you gazed with reverence at a wild flower, a grain of sand?*

- *Is the experience of eternity foreign or familiar to you?*

- *Yes, how much do you know about God?*

Praying with the Church

> Father,
> may we whom you renew in baptism
> bear witness to our faith by the way we live.
> By the suffering, death, and resurrection of your Son
> may we come to eternal joy.
> We ask this through our Lord Jesus Christ, your Son,
> who lives and reigns with you and the Holy Spirit,
> one God, for ever and ever.

Week Five

FIFTH SUNDAY of EASTER

John 14:1–12 (A); John 15:1–8 (B); John 13:31–33, 34–35 (C)

FEAR AND LOVE don't mix well, like oil and water. But then it all depends on what type of fear we are talking about, what type of love. Perfect love does cast out all foolish fear. Yet our hearts are often troubled by the anxieties of life, frightened of the glory of God, worried that we, weak and barren branches, might be severed from the vine. So we must choose and hopefully we will turn to the risen Lord as the way, the truth, and the life. Any other choice throws us into the darkness of destructive fear.

Refrain: Whoever lives in me and I in him will yield much fruit, says the Lord, alleluia.

PEOPLE TELL ME

People tell me "Don't be afraid of God,
for God is Love."
O don't you see
I fear the very Lover
in my God!

I fear the Lover
hiding glory in drab disguise
of humble people

I fear the Lover
barely daring to reveal
his gentle breeze of being
lest majesty beget
tremendous homage

I fear the one who loves me
and touches with such tenderness
this fragile thing of freedom that is "me"
lest it be shattered

and yet perhaps I have no fear of God
but of his being Love
and so of me

I fear the fact that he is Love and so
must leave me all the drama of decision
that love requires

            — as sure as light reveals
and darkness veils, I too much choose
the narrow way, the holocaust, the bleak
leap of abandonment into the barely known
and yet demanding deep —
I fear the fact that I am made to choose
and so may lose

Ralph Wright, O.S.B.

The psalmist tells us that the beginning of wisdom is fear. Other people tell us that we should not be afraid, afraid of God who is Love and Mercy and Compassion. In our more honest moments we all have fears: of God, of the dark, of the unknown, of the hidden abyss of existence. Too often our apparent courage is thin-voiced bravado.

In truth we should fear God's powerful glory, God's overwhelming tenderness, God's extravagant kindness. Yet we pray for a graced fear, one filled with reverence and awe. This gift of the Holy Spirit draws us closer to the divine sanctuary. Unlike cowardly or subservient fear, this holy trepidation shatters our pride and clothes us in humility.

At bottom our fear confronts our freedom. We must choose within the limitations of our narrow knowledge and paltry love. Given these restrictions we are in danger of making the wrong choice and we have here good cause for fear. But even here we turn to God in trust and faith, assured that the risen Lord will give us sufficient grace.

- *What are your three major fears?*

- *Listen attentively to the Lord speaking to you this Sunday: "Peace be with you! Have no fear for I am near!"*

- *How does love cast out fear in your life?*

Praying with the Church

> Father of our Lord Jesus Christ,
> you have revealed to the nations your saving power
> and filled all ages with the words of a new song.
> Hear the echo of this hymn.

Give us voice to sing your praise
through this season of joy.
We ask this through Christ our Lord.

MONDAY of the FIFTH WEEK of EASTER
John 14:21–26

TWO DISEASES that plague our human journey are ignorance
and forgetfulness. Often we simply do not know how loved
we are and what dignity has been given to us. Often we forget
the word of God and fail to put it into practice. But we live on
hope, on a promise made by God that the Spirit will instruct us
and remind us of what is really important in life. Our responsibility is to respond, to say yes to God's instructions and reminders.
When we do this, we come to the realization that God truly
dwells within us.

*Refrain: Whoever loves me will be loved by my Father, and I will
love him and show myself to him, alleluia.*

ALTHOUGH DUST

Although dust
I am loved
by the one
eternal
Son of the Father

just as intensely
as this same Father
loves this one
eternal Son

O mystery
O majesty
O wonder
that what we
in our wildest dreams
could not conceive
has been
by God's own Word
quietly revealed

Ralph Wright, O.S.B.

Humility is foundational to the Christian life. We know that we are dust, and unto dust we shall all return. Yet in the poverty of the human condition we also know in faith that we are loved with an intensity comparable to the inner love of the Trinity. Indeed, all is grace and our response to this mystery should be one of gratitude and praise.

We all have dreams, some wild, some tame. But even in our wildest dreams no one could possibly conceive of a triune God who has become incarnate and who continues to guide us still through the gift of the Holy Spirit. The mysteries of the Trinity and incarnation exceed our finite reason, even our far-ranging imagination. Yet we are surrounded and immersed in these mysteries that continue to enlighten and nourish us.

Faith empowers us to embrace revelation. Through this theo-logical virtue we come to the radical conviction of God's love and mercy that sustains and surrounds all of us. It is a quiet revelation happening in the dead of night underneath a brilliant star, and another that happens before dawn when people discover an empty tomb. Christmas and Easter are our revelatory feast days. O mystery, O majesty, O supreme wonder!

- *How do you experience God's love?*

- *During this Easter season what revelations have come your way?*

- *In your wildest dreams, what is your vision of happiness?*

Praying with the Church

> Father,
> help us to seek the values
> that will bring us eternal joy in this changing world.
> In our desire for what you promise
> make us one in mind and heart.
> Grant this through our Lord Jesus Christ, your Son,
> who lives and reigns with you and the Holy Spirit,
> one God, for ever and ever.

TUESDAY of the FIFTH WEEK of EASTER
John 14:27–31

S T. PAUL lists nine signs of the Holy Spirit (Galatians 5:22). Peace is one of them and, when experienced, greatly reduces the distress and fear that is part of human existence. God whispers peace to us in a variety of ways: through the sacraments, especially reconciliation; through the exercise of virtue, the doing of good; through the community, as people reveal God to us through deeds of love and kindness. The visitations of our loving God are daily affairs and will be noticed and responded to if our faith is deep.

Refrain: Peace I leave with you, alleluia; peace is my gift to you, alleluia.

PEOPLE WHISPER GOD TO ME

People whisper God to me
far more than mountains
for landscape beauty bores —
however roaring or majestic
is the pageant music
played behind
their massive faces
sunsets have no sympathy
and — for all its background
awe-inspiring paintwash —
granite cannot smile.

Ralph Wright, O.S.B.

Mountains and oceans, simply by their massiveness, whisper something of the divine to us. So too sunsets that paint the western sky in purples and pinks, filling our evenings with beauty. Then there is granite, solid and "eternal," hinting of permanence in an ever changing world.

Yet our souls hunger for two simple gifts: sympathy and a smile. Whenever we find an empathetic heart, whenever we feel the compassion of a fellow-sufferer, our loneliness is lessened and we hear in these experiences the love of God. And a smile is so powerful that it can, as Albert Schweitzer maintains, "stay a suicide." A smile of affirmation endorses our dignity, giving us a sense of worth.

Mountains and sunsets and granite lack the capacity for compassion and affirmation. They know no sympathy; they are incapable of smiling. But people whisper God to us because they can enter into our experience and rejoice in our victories and cry with us in our sorrows. People have the potential for smiling and transmitting the love that God has given to them. Throughout this Easter season we are challenged to hear people whisper God to us; we are challenged to whisper God to others.

- *Can smiling be an intentional activity?*

- *What is your degree of sympathy, especially toward the poor?*

- *To whom will you whisper God today?*

Praying with the Church

> Father,
> you restored your people to eternal life
> by raising Christ your Son from death.
> Make our faith strong and our hope sure.

May we never doubt that you will fulfill
the promises you have made.
Grant this through our Lord Jesus Christ, your Son,
who lives and reigns with you and the Holy Spirit,
one God, for ever and ever.

WEDNESDAY of the FIFTH WEEK
John 15:1–8

WE LIVE ON IMAGES AND METAPHORS that offer us a vision
of identity and destiny. Jesus describes himself as a vine,
in other places as a shepherd and friend. Each of these symbols
manifests some aspect of our Lord's life: as vine he is the source
of our life and fruitfulness; as shepherd he is the one who protects
and guides us; as friend, Jesus reveals to us the secrets of his heart
and mission. It has been claimed that in every autobiography
there is a central metaphor that offers a sense of identity. During
this Easter season we return again to the question, who are we?

Refrain: I am the true vine, alleluia, you are the branches, alleluia.

I AM A SHELL

I am a shell
listen to me
for the roar and silence
of the eternal sea.
Ralph Wright, O.S.B.

The poet identifies himself as a shell. One implication here is a hollowness or emptiness that seeks to be filled. One defining characteristic of Christian anthropology is the awareness of our intrinsic poverty, our radical indigence. Likewise, the vine is attached to the branch; everything that comes its way is gift. Unless something or someone outside gives it substance or nourishment, it remains in the state of barrenness.

The shell asks to be listened to. The vine longs to transmit what it is receiving into some type of fruitfulness. In these images we seek the essence of life caught up in the dynamic of receiving and giving. If the shell is not empty, the listener hears nothing; if there is no branch, the vine withers and dies. Shells and vines and humans are conduits that channel sounds and life and love to those who hunger for meaning, wholeness, and intimacy.

The shell depends upon the sea for sound and silence. All life must be seen in terms of relationships. In a sense the shell is a disciple of the sea just as we are disciples of a risen Master. To the extent that we listen to the divine Teacher will we transmit to those who listen to us the roar of God's love and the silence of divine mercy. In this way we will bear much fruit, fruit that will last.

- *What images, biblical or otherwise, give you a sense of identity?*

- *Does the imagery of the vine and branches speak to your experience?*

- *What fruit are you bearing during this Easter season?*

Praying with the Church

> Father of all holiness,
> guide our hearts to you.

Keep in the light of your truth
all those you have freed from the darkness of unbelief.
We ask this through our Lord Jesus Christ, your Son
who lives and reigns with you and the Holy Spirit,
one God, for ever and ever.

THURSDAY of the FIFTH WEEK of EASTER
John 15:9–11

A JOY NOT SHARED is incomplete. The way in which joy is experienced is through the mystery of love. Within the Trinity we are told of the mutual love between the Father and the Son. Within the mystery of the incarnation we see revealed the love of God for humankind. There is a double joy here: triune joy overflowing into creation, human joy known in living the command of love.

Refrain: If you keep my commandments, you will live in my love, alleluia.

WHEN I WRITE

when I write
of the joy
of life with God

I think of you
being
for that moment
one with me

then I wonder
why that moment
ever ended
and I long
for when it won't

Ralph Wright, O.S.B.

Writing is a form of communication that reduces the distance between correspondents. Though geographic miles are not decreased, the letter sent is an assurance that one is thought of and cared for. The intimacy of writing is deepened when the subject matter is our life in God, our participation in the mystery of holiness. There is much joy here.

Too quickly the successiveness of time cuts short this desire for eternal joy. The passion and feeling refuse to remain stationary and life moves on to other events and other emotions. But the desire for permanence remains firm as does the hope that one day neither joy nor intimacy will cease. The term "forever" has been planted in the human heart and until it germinates and bears fruit we will be restless.

Unlike phone calls, letters stay to be looked at, reread, folded neatly in one's special drawer. Time and time again we can go back to the "I love you" or "Miss you so much" or "You are forever in my heart." Joy can be reborn again and again as we ponder the mystery of love that God has embedded in our souls. Perhaps this Easter season we would do well to write someone of the joy of life with God.

- *What is the quality of your correspondence? Do you ever write about our joy in God?*

- *Do you have a "keeper" file for special letters that tell of deep things?*

- *How can you be an instrument of God's joy today?*

Praying with the Church

> Father, in your love you have brought us
> from evil to good and from misery to happiness.
> Through your blessings
> give the courage of perseverance
> to those you have called and justified by faith.
> Grant this through our Lord Jesus Christ, your Son,
> who lives and reigns with you and the Holy Spirit,
> one God, for ever and ever.

FRIDAY of the FIFTH WEEK of EASTER
John 15:12–17

MIRRORS DO NOT LIE except at the circus. And even there, no matter what the degree of distortion, there is still some similarity to the original. As we look into the word of God and hear about love and friendship, our challenge is to reflect Jesus' love in today's world. Our friendship with God empowers us to bear fruit that will sustain others on this long human journey. All of this is possible because we have been chosen and called to be instruments of grace.

Refrain: My commandment is this: love one another as I have loved you, alleluia.

I Looked into the Mirror

I looked into the mirror
and saw your face
in all its beauty

you knocked
I said "Come in" turned
and in your face
I saw myself
while you said
"Have you become
my twin?"
and we laughed

such are the jokes
of lovers

Ralph Wright, O.S.B.

Jokes are holy because they make us laugh and enter into the presence of joy. How can people, born so many years before, become twins? Who is kidding whom? Yet, it is possible over time to so identify with the values and attitudes of others that we do become spiritual and psychological twins, seeing the same things, thinking the same thoughts, feeling the same passions. Such is the power of friendship and affinity.

Jesus calls his disciples, not slaves, but friends. There is a deep love that bonds them together in the same mission of doing the Father's will. Jesus sees himself in the faces of the disciples and they in turn discover the Lord's countenance in their own. Such is the bonding that now they are willing to die for each other, the sign of supreme friendship and commitment.

Beauty and laughter are signs of the Holy Spirit. Beauty emerges out of harmonious relationships and laughter explodes as we see the gaps between what we are and what we would like to be. Lovers live in the presence of mutual beauty and laugh at the practical jokes that keep them human. Loving one another as the Lord has loved us is a thing of beauty and great cause for laughing joy.

- *Would it be irreverent to see the resurrection appearances as forms of joking?*

- *Do you have a spiritual twin?*

- *When you look into the mirror do you ever see anyone else?*

Praying with the Church

> Lord,
> by this Easter mystery
> prepare us for eternal life.
> May our celebration of Christ's death and resurrection
> guide us to salvation.
> We ask this through our Lord Jesus Christ, your Son,
> who lives and reigns with you and the Holy Spirit,
> one God, for ever and ever.

SATURDAY of the FIFTH WEEK of EASTER
John 15:18–21

L OVE AND AGGRESSION are two fundamental instincts in human nature. Jesus speaks directly to both of them when he says that we will be hated when we refuse to go along with false values. In his own life Jesus experienced violent rejection through his crucifixion. It is not surprising that his disciples should also expect similar rejection when they follow in the way of love, compassion, and forgiveness. Stephen, an early Church martyr, was willing to pay the price.

Refrain: Christ died and rose from the dead, that he might be the Lord of the living and the dead, alleluia.

STEPHEN

they killed him as one kills a wasp,
treading, crushing, stamping
— or against a window with a book —
while he was praying forgive them

they needed him gone quickly
before he could escape
and in his anger sting the world
with the Carpenter's love
that leaves all naked

Ralph Wright, O.S.B.

Two moments in scripture that astound the human heart: to hear Jesus from the cross and Stephen in the midst of being stoned praying that their persecutors might be forgiven. At the natural level we seek revenge in the face of injury; at the level of grace we recognize ignorance on the part of persecutors and pray that mercy be shown them. One wonders what went on in the heart of Saul, later St. Paul, as he approved at what was being done.

Wasps sting and inflict sharp pain. But when we are stung by love we are given the vaccine of life. Stephen in his encounter with death gave life just as Jesus died that he might rise to eternal life. This event that we call the paschal mystery leaves the mind and heart naked, uncovered, unable to comprehend so deep a truth. No explanations satisfy. Reason is left behind as faith rushes to embrace the truth of mystery.

Why is it that history is filled with so much killing and violence? Why should we fear the "Carpenter's love"? Perhaps it is because we then must surrender ourselves to a life of praise and thanksgiving, a life demanding a full and total response to God's self-giving love. Too many of us will have to leave too many things and attitudes and illusions behind. Thus the messengers that come to call us to truth and freedom will continually risk their lives in our presence.

- *Do you pray that those who oppose you or hurt you be forgiven?*

- *Is the "Carpenter's love" operative in your heart?*

- *Have you ever persecuted anyone for telling the truth?*

Praying with the Church

> Loving Father,
> through our rebirth in baptism
> you give us your life and promise immortality.
> By your unceasing care,
> guide our steps toward the life of glory.
> Grant this through our Lord Jesus Christ, your Son,
> who lives and reigns with you and the Holy Spirit,
> one God, for ever and ever.

EASTER SEASON

Week Six

SIXTH SUNDAY of EASTER

John 14:15–21 (A); John 15:9–17 (B); John 14:23–29 (C)

SUNDAY IS THE DAY that we Christians celebrate again and again the great mystery of the resurrection. Jesus, the son of God, continues to shine upon us with the warmth and graciousness of God's love. Sunday after Sunday we expose ourselves to the message of love and are invited to deepen our participation in the paschal mystery. Even nature enters into the cycle of dying and rising and becomes a constant reminder of the fidelity of the sun and the Son.

Refrain: As the Father has loved me, so I have loved you; live on in my love, alleluia.

IN AN HOUR OF SUN

The Wisconsin winter hung on
and on, snow after Easter,
nights down to frost and freezing.
Then in an hour of welcome sun,
I raked leaves from ten feet
of flower borders, careful

with tulips' pointed leaves,
the patch of tender mallow,
a spiky beginning of poppies.
Stooping to pull dead grass
from a clump of wild violets
I find five blooming crocus,
a forgotten autumn planting,
their purple flowers celebrating
all the garden's little resurrections.

Helen Fahrbach

The spiritual life has its seasons, one of which is winter. When things interior are cold and dark we may be tempted to question whether spring will ever come again. Snow covers the earth, the sun fails to provide sufficient light and warmth, and the freezing wind blowing in our faces with hostility and apparent anger gives us the impression that life itself is against us.

But beneath the appearance of lifelessness, God's love continues to give life at deep levels. God's promise of presence and new life becomes the source of our confidence and hope. Trust is needed in these fallow months and, more than trust, a personal discipline to rake away the debris that covers those small seeds of grace that seek to break forth in new life.

Even in the midst of winter there are little resurrections. These may be manifest in the gift of flowers from a loved one, in a passage of scripture that stirs the heart, in the suffering that opens us to new levels of compassion, in the call to patience that prepares us for new and deeper graces. Because of Jesus, death does not have the final word. His love is immortal and his presence is assured. We need but open our souls to Easter faith.

- *Have you had any little or large resurrections this Easter season?*

- *Is gardening a spiritual exercise for you?*

- *What season are you now living in: spring? summer? autumn? winter?*

Praying with the Church

> God our Father, maker of all,
> the crown of your creation was the Son of Man,
> born of woman, but without beginning;
> he suffered for us but lives forever.
> May our mortal lives be crowned with the ultimate joy
> of rising with him,
> who is Lord for ever and ever.

MONDAY of the SIXTH WEEK of EASTER
John 15:26–16:4

IN HIS GRACIOUSNESS, Jesus prepares the disciples for his absence. Soon he will no longer be with them, and they will have to endure that anguish of grief and sadness. Though trials and sufferings will come, Jesus promises to send the Spirit to empower them to witness to the truth and embrace the cross. Following Jesus involves both winter and spring, both death and life. Our baptism draws us full circle into God's love.

Refrain: By raising Jesus Christ from the dead, God has given us a new birth to a living hope in the promise of an inheritance that will last forever, alleluia.

FULL CIRCLE

Your absence haunts every season,
the ravel of memories
strewing my dreams
like dormant flowers
buried under an unforgiving snow.

When winter slows with the spurt
of crocus pushing up,
the green of spring
is too far away to bring comfort.

I long for the burst
of bleeding hearts and tulips,
beds of columbine
overgrown and wild.

I plan the garden of summer
knowing I alone will dig and plant
and wonder if autumn's fires
will burn grief, the winter winds
scatter the ashes.

Helen Fahrbach

Longing is a human characteristic of extreme importance. Our desires and longings reveal our heart and also indicate what is missing in our lives. One of our deepest yearnings is for fullness of life; another is for companionship. What grief is felt when a loved one dies, when a master leaves his disciples. It's as if the heart has been pierced by an invisible sword and refuses to heal.

Jesus' Spirit is one of fire and wind. When the disciples once again felt the fire ("were not our hearts burning within us?"), their former grief vanished. They were able now to leave the paralyzing field of sorrow and reach out to others in proclaiming new life. The Spirit is also one of wind that both scatters the ashes of grief and energizes us to move beyond pain to the season of summer. All our trust is in the promise Jesus makes to us about his abiding presence.

On the human level we sometimes have to dig and plant alone when a partner dies. Such is not the case on the spiritual journey. Jesus does not leave us orphaned but continues to plan and plant, cultivate and harvest the garden within us. Surely the disciples missed the historical Jesus and the sound of his familiar voice and the gaze of his love. But they knew that the risen Christ dwelt within them and worked with them every step of the way.

- *How do you deal with grief?*

- *What is your sense of presence regarding God's role in your life?*

- *What part does Jesus play in planning and planting your spiritual garden?*

Praying with the Church

> God of mercy,
> may our celebration of your Son's resurrection
> help us to experience its effect in our lives.
> We ask this through our Lord Jesus Christ, your Son,
> who lives and reigns with you and the Holy Spirit,
> one God, for ever and ever.

TUESDAY of the SIXTH WEEK of EASTER
John 16:5–11

THE SOBER TRUTH is that we all must die, that one day we go away from one another. Jesus explained that his imminent death was necessary if the Holy Spirit was to come, a Spirit that would prove the values of the world to be erroneous regarding grace and sin, justice and equality, salvation and condemnation. One senses that the disciples were not convinced that it would be better for Jesus to go and for the Paraclete to come. These followers were overwhelmed by grief as Jesus' departure drew near.

Refrain: In a little while the world will no longer see me, but you will see me, for I live and you will live, alleluia.

WHEN SOMEONE DIES IN MAY

> All strings that hold
> the heart in place
> pull tighter as spring winds
> carry tears
> of mourning women

who grieve,
long for daughters
to sing birthing songs,
to place their hands
like small birds
on their mother's hair
and braid comfort.

Helen Fahrbach

The human heart is a land of great mystery. The joys and griefs that pass through the interior regions of our being are most difficult to describe, though easily felt. The news of death tightens the heart, causing physical and psychological pain. And when the death involves one's flesh and blood it is almost incredible that one can survive the blow. Mothers, in particular, suffer extreme sorrow when their children die.

Since spoken words are so inadequate to carry the depths of the heart's joys and sorrows, we humans break into songs of jubilation or dirges that express the silent tears of the soul. Indeed, we prefer birthing songs, songs of life and victory, but death and loss force us into mournful strains.

Preference means nothing here. We must sing the truth before us and pray that the melody, whatever its key or motif, will see us through because we sing together.

Scriptures remind us that there is a time for everything, a time to love and to hate, a time to plant and harvest, a time to rejoice and a time to cry. Braided comfort sometimes is not possible because the hands of the beloved cannot be present. One day, in faith, the mourning will cease and the morning of God's comfort and compassion will break upon us like the dawn.

- *What songs have you sung or have you heard in times of loss?*

- *Is there a false comfort that is offered too soon or too easily in moments of tragedy?*

- *Are you able to feel your heart's strings?*

Praying with the Church

> God our Father,
> may we look forward with hope to our resurrection,
> for you have made us your sons and daughters,
> and restored the joy of our youth.
> We ask this through our Lord Jesus Christ, your Son,
> who lives and reigns with you and the Holy Spirit,
> one God, for ever and ever.

WEDNESDAY of the SIXTH WEEK of EASTER
John 16:12–15

THE PROMISE OF THE HOLY SPIRIT is the promise of truth. Jesus experienced the truth of his being at the Jordan river when the "dove" descended upon him with the assuring conviction that he, Jesus, was the beloved of the Father. Throughout history that song of the joyful dove coos of God's love to all who join Jesus at the baptismal waters. We need but repent and believe in order to hear that song and regain our integrity. When that happens the dawn will find us rejoicing.

Refrain: I have many more things to tell you, but they would be too much for you now. When the Spirit of truth comes he will guide you to all truth, alleluia.

As the Mourning Dove Sings It

That mourning dove out there
is working on a sad song
about yesterday and how
today may bring more sorrow,
the monotonous low tones
repeating the grey sky. Perhaps she's

only calling for a mate or
comforting small hungry doves,
her muted feathers
hidden in the dim gloom of the hedge,
her persistent mournful notes the only
clue to shape, but the pause
between verses begs me to listen.

Helen Fahrbach

During the Easter season we are challenged to be good listeners. God continues to speak to us in so many ways: the song of birds, the hymns of our liturgies, the diverse melodies of daily existence. In between the verses we have that wonderful silent space to find meaning and come to the truth of things. The Spirit works in sound and silence, in action and contemplation, in seasons of comfort and desolation. We strain to listen to the message that will guide us in God's direction.

Through its mournful notes, the mourning dove reminds us that something is missing in our lives. Our minds are made for infinite wisdom, our hearts for extravagant love. Even the best of our human learning and the greatest of our friendships cannot fill our deepest hungers and thirsts.

Augustine's famous "our hearts are restless till they rest in thee" tells us the reason that our soul is in mourning.

But we need not focus on the half-filled glass. Our vessels are more than half-filled and the Spirit of truth and joy has been given to us. While keenly aware of what is not yet, our faith tells us that we have been given so much. There is great cause for rejoicing both in present grace of the Spirit's working and in the promise of more to come. We might well sing back to the mourning dove a joyful song.

- *How has the Spirit of truth and joy touched your life?*

- *Do you tend, by way of temperament, to see the glass half-full or half-empty?*

- *What is the tone of your mourning song?*

Praying with the Church

> Lord,
> as we celebrate your Son's resurrection,
> so may we rejoice with all the saints
> when he returns in glory,
> who lives and reigns with you and the Holy Spirit,
> one God, for ever and ever.

THURSDAY of the SIXTH WEEK of EASTER
John 16:16–20

J ESUS' RELATIONSHIP with his disciples has a definite pattern. Forever the teacher, Jesus instructs the disciples in the way of the cross. It is through the mystery of death that life is given; it is in dying to the self that one truly lives; it is in giving away everything that we gain all. The disciples did not understand until the final lesson when Jesus died on Calvary and rose to new life. This pattern, this paschal mystery of dying and rising, is reflected both in our faith and even in nature. Our task is to enter into this pattern with passion and follow Jesus through the cross into his resurrection.

Refrain: In a little while you will no longer see me, says the Lord; then a little while later you will see me again, since I am going to the Father, alleluia.

PATTERNS

Today wild phlox bloom purple
in a stream of sun drifts of daisies
breathe a white promise of summer

But yesterday death visited the garden
I found a scatter of feathers
a decapitated sparrow on the path
small brown mouse wet with rain
cold and broken under the bleeding heart

Patterns keep repeating life like a flower
common as marigolds death that comes
carrying a huddle of grief and loneliness

Helen Fahrbach

It's a matter of life and death, so the saying goes. All of existence is involved in this process of being born, growing, and dying. Feelings of grief and loneliness criss-cross the human heart as, season after season, it experiences new life and tragic death. Even flowers, for all their sweetness, smell of mortality.

But there is something more here than just the promise of summer and a vision of an autumn harvest. The promise that Jesus makes is one of eternal life. Sin and death have been broken once and for all through the sacrificial love of the cross. Scattered feathers, headless sparrows, mice on the verge of extinction cannot destroy the hope that life will one day triumph over death.

Living a virtuous life is the pattern that does involve dying and rising all the way through life. It is the pattern that Mary lived when she said yes to the will of God; it is the pattern that Jesus taught in parables regarding grains of wheat; it is the pattern that all of us are invited into through our baptism. If we die with the Lord, we shall indeed rise with him. It is the mystery of the resurrection that comes bearing the light of joy and belonging.

- *What are three of the basic patterns in your life (eating patterns? reading patterns? speaking patterns?)?*

- *In what season do you experience a greater promise of inner growth?*

- *How do you participate in the pattern of the paschal mystery?*

Praying with the Church

> Father,
> may we always give you thanks
> for raising Christ our Lord to glory,
> because we are his people

and share the salvation he won,
for he lives and reigns with you and the Holy Spirit,
one God, for ever and ever.

FRIDAY of the SIXTH WEEK of EASTER
John 16:20–23

SOME JOYS IN OUR LIFE are short-lived. Within a half hour the sunset has slipped away; all too soon the trophy becomes tarnished, if not lost; even the joy of physical agility must yield to diminishment. But there is a joy that lasts forever: the joy of love. Thus even as a mother endures the pain of delivery, her love for the child she has carried these many months provides the courage to embrace the hardship. Though Jesus departs from his disciples with his mission accomplished, the grief of farewell gives way to the joy of the risen life and a new form of presence that insures the fullness of life.

Refrain: Because he suffered death, we see Jesus crowned with glory and honor, alleluia.

WATCHING BIRDS

They gather around the feeders
searching for daily bread,

juncos perching in the lilacs,
house finches, a flutter of wings.

The garden's alive this winter
with feasting and music all day,

and I keep my eyes on the sparrow,
on the stem in the mouth of a dove.

Helen Fahrbach

Like birds, all of us search for our daily bread. This hunger is for more than mere physical sustenance. It is a passion for love and joy that we find in the person of Jesus Christ. Our watching and waiting goes far beyond the beauties of nature — be they birds or flowers or rolling meadows. Our eyes yearn to see the face of the living God and experience the joy of the divine glance.

We associate resurrection and Easter with spring. But the life of the risen Lord cannot be limited to a single season. Even in winter there is feasting and music because the Lord is near. Cold north winds and freezing temperatures do not discourage us. Just as the garden is alive with the banqueting and melodies of winter birds so the warmth of our fireplaces encourages storytelling and human bonding. The garden of creation is alive because our God not only creates and sustains existence; our God continues to redeem and sanctify it through the mystery of Jesus and the gift of the Holy Spirit.

It is good to keep our eyes open to the flight of the sparrow, to the feeding habits of the dove. Bird watching is a marvelous hobby because it makes us pay attention. If we are alert to the things of nature, we are practicing the art of being alert to another dove, the Dove of the Holy Spirit, who hovers over us and offers gracious warmth. In our seeing we are also seen, and in that is the fullness of our joy.

- *Do you bird watch? Do you watch for the coming of the Spirit?*

- *What is the source of your daily bread?*

- *Is winter a season alive to you with feasting and music?*

Praying with the Church

> Lord,
> hear our prayer
> that your Gospel may reach all people
> and that we who receive salvation through your Word
> may be your children in deed as well as in name.
> We ask this through our Lord Jesus Christ, your Son,
> who lives and reigns with you and the Holy Spirit,
> one God, for ever and ever.

SATURDAY of the SIXTH WEEK of EASTER
John 16:23–28

ASKING CAN GO in one of two directions: asking to receive and asking to give. What is it that we ask of God? More money, better positions, greater esteem? Or do some ask of God the grace to be agents of truth and love in a world that is dark with ignorance and cold with indifference? When we approach the altar, surely we come not only with our petitions for our many needs but also laden with our simple gifts of bread and wine, with our ordinary duties performed out of love, with our commitment to follow more closely the way of Jesus.

Refrain: I promise that the Father will give you anything you ask in my name, alleluia.

AN ORDINARY TASK

Like a handmaiden devoted
to her duties I begin my task,
mindful of every moment.

Hands comforted in steaming suds
I grasp the slender stem of wineglass,
dinner plates, cups and saucers.

Each dish is laved, rinsed, and dried,
my kitchen counter like an altar
covered with holy vessels.

Helen Fahrbach

In our Christian tradition, Mary is the handmaiden who lived a life of mindfulness. Her task was to hear God's word, conceive it in her heart, and give it birth in her daily life. This is what she asked of the Lord: "Be it done according to your will." Her heart was like an altar which held the mystery of obedience and self-giving. Hers was a eucharistic life.

In our hurried culture, unfriendly toward the basic duties of life, we need again to commit ourselves to finding God in the ordinary tasks of daily existence. Courtesy on the phone, full hospitality to an unexpected guest, a smile across the subway aisle and, yes, the doing of dishes at the sink can all be epiphanies of faith. God visits us every hour of every day. Those who are mindful open their hearts and respond with love.

Each of us has his or her own altar, even those who profess no faith. And on that altar we place our vessels, some of which are holy and others are not. We bring our vessels of simplicity or greed, our containers of gentleness or violence, our repository of hope or despair. We human creatures are made to be worshipers and our freedom dictates what the object/subject of our worship will be. In faith we bring back to the Lord the gift God has given to us: our ordinary, extraordinary lives.

- *What is your degree of mindfulness this day?*

- *What are the ordinary tasks God has assigned to you?*

- *What gifts do you bring to the altar?*

Praying for the Church

> Lord,
> teach us to know you better
> by doing good to others.
> Help us to grow in your love
> and come to understand the eternal mystery
> of Christ's death and resurrection.
> We ask this through our Lord Jesus Christ, your Son,
> who lives and reigns with you and the Holy Spirit,
> one God, for ever and ever.

EASTER SEASON

Week Seven

SEVENTH SUNDAY of EASTER
John 17:1–11 (A); John 17:11–19 (B); John 17:20–26 (C)

THE INTIMACY between Jesus and his Father is partially revealed in this seventeenth chapter of John's Gospel. But
there is another intimacy also disclosed: the intimacy between
Jesus and his disciples. We witness in the life of Jesus the balance
between the horizontal and vertical dimensions of our faith. Our
love must have a double direction, one pointing to the transcendent mystery of God and the other to our sisters and brothers
who are the immanent mystery surrounding us. Glory happens
when our love is full and inclusive, like Jesus' love.

*Refrain: Father, I have glorified you upon the earth, I have accom-
plished the work you gave me to do, alleluia.*

FAITH

When faith senses a promise it looks like hope.
When faith burns like fire we call it love.
This pearl of great price makes us rich
in the things of God and eternity.

This gem, both rare and common,
is strewn along each human pathway.
Yet, strange, no ownership can be claimed.
Faith, a gift freely given
and nightly lost.
Each morning we ask anew for the promise and presence.
Then we walk again the road of hope and love.

Robert F. Morneau

The theological virtues — faith, hope, charity — are special gifts that "connect" us in diverse ways with our God. Faith focuses on the very Being of God; hope leads us to trustful reliance on God's many promises; charity inflames our hearts with a love that will never end. In praying for his disciples (and for us — now!), Jesus continues the work that was given him by his Father.

Our work has to do with the glory of God. And God is glorified when we live according to God's plan, that is, when we love his Son, when we believe and hope. Unfortunately, the obstacles to this growth are many and have a long history. Faith confronts doubt that can be as persistent as a summer fly; hope must encounter moments and months of despair; charity faces the demons of indifference and apathy that paralyze our hearts.

Faith is a free gift. Each dawn we must again ask for this grace and resolve to live it as deeply as possible. With this gift we can venture into the future assured that God will be faithful to divine promises and we will experience the fire of the Spirit enkindling our hearts to burn with concern for others. And if our personal prayer falters, we know that Jesus sits at the Father's right hand interceding for us at this very moment.

- *How do you plan to "glorify" God this next week?*

- *How does your faith impact on your hope and love?*

- *What "work" has God given you to do in this life?*

Praying with the Church

> Eternal Father,
> reaching from end to end of the universe,
> and ordering all things with your mighty arm:
> for you, time is the unfolding of truth that already is,
> the unveiling of beauty that is yet to be.
> Your Son has saved us in history
> by rising from the dead,
> so that transcending time he might free us from death.
> May his presence among us
> lead to the vision of unlimited truth
> and unfold the beauty of your love.
> We ask this in the name of Jesus the Lord.

MONDAY of the SEVENTH WEEK of EASTER
John 16:29–33

ONE THING ABOUT FAITH that is certain — it cannot exist long beside arrogance. The disciples (all of them speaking or Peter alone?) are sure of their convictions and need not ask any more questions. Our faith cannot rely on "unveiled language" nor on our personal convictions. Jesus warns of tough days to come when this bold faith will prove cowardly. Once again the disciples are being instructed not to trust in themselves but rather in the peace that is promised to those who follow the Lord.

Refrain: The world will persecute you, but have courage, I have overcome the world, alleluia.

THE TINGLE OF LIFE

It happens, that mysterious surge of energy
lightning down the spine with chilling heat.
It happened on hearing Hopkins'
    "...dearest freshness deep down things"
and being grasped by the Australian Southern Cross
and smelling the mowing of the June hay.
Perhaps we are still vulnerable to the shiver,
to the electrical wonder of nature
and the mystical awe of the divine.
Perhaps, but only if we refuse immunity from humanity,
and expose ourselves to Beauty that lovingly shocks us awake.
Yesterday my soul tingled, shivered, was stirred,
and I knew I was alive.

Robert F. Morneau

In Psychology 101 we learn almost in the first class the many forms of defense mechanisms that float through our psyche protecting our fragile ego. Rationalization is one, repression another, the illusion of invulnerability a third. Few of us heed the advice of old, mad King Lear: "Expose thyself to what the wretches feel." We would rather live protected from life's harm.

The danger of this choice is that we close ourselves to the possibility of experiencing the good as well as the difficult in life. Hidden away in our defensiveness and fear is the powerful line of a poem, or the marvel of a starry constellation, or the graced seduction of nature. Being invulnerable to the bad carries a heavy price tag: we become invulnerable to the good as well. We must take courage and follow in the humanity of Jesus.

Jesus was stirred when he saw the sorrow of a grieving widow; Jesus shivered in the dark garden as his betrayer and his band approached; Jesus experienced the tingle of joy in the company of children and in partaking of wine at a wedding. Jesus was fully alive to all of life and invites us to experience the peace that such a way of life brings. Jesus overcomes the world by tasting deeply its depths. This offers evidence that Jesus truly comes from God.

- *When was the last time a shiver ran down your spine?*

- *What types of immunity do you seek?*

- *How can you expose yourself to Beauty this week? Art museum? Concert? Walk in nature?*

Praying with the Church

> Lord,
> send the power of your Holy Spirit upon us
> that we may remain faithful
> and do your will in our daily lives.
> We ask this through our Lord Jesus Christ, your Son,
> who lives and reigns with you and the Holy Spirit,
> one God, for ever and ever.

TUESDAY of the SEVENTH WEEK of EASTER
John 17:1–11

THE MISSION OF JESUS involved making God known. Two ways dominated his methodology: (1) doing what he saw the Father doing — loving and forgiving; and (2) teaching the truth so as to dispel the darkness of ignorance. By living love and instructing others in the ways of wisdom Jesus gave glory to God. We have been baptized into the same mission of Jesus; we have been called to give glory to God. By living the Gospel and passing on the message of Jesus we are graced into eternal life.

Refrain: The Lord has risen from the dead as he promised; let all the earth rejoice and be glad, for he shall reign forever, alleluia.

HEARSAY

I've heard it said that
    death devastates the human heart   and that
    love liberates imprisoned souls   and that
    God hides in burning bushes and soft breezes.
All hearsay some say.

My sister, brother, niece buried in our village cemetery
  — a part of my heart entombed there too.

My soul set free by glances of love
  — summer graces — sheer gift.

My faith, long dormant and untended
  — now aflame given God's gracious name.

Hearsay? Others telling of God and love and death?

Now having seen and been touched by Mystery,

I say...!

Robert F. Morneau

Some people have never seen a prairie or a sea and have to rely on others for their knowledge and description of them. Some people have never received love nor encountered friendship and they can only guess at the accuracy of essays written on these topics. Still other individuals are ignorant of war, some of peace, and hearsay is their only resource for learning.

But all of us have had first-hand encounters with the sun and rain, with sin and pain, with fears and dreams. When we can speak from personal experience ("I say..."), we need not rely on second-hand accounts. We each have our story to tell of how our souls and the mystery of life intersect.

Then there is the God experience. All hearsay? All derived knowledge from the mystics and saints? Or is the risen Lord near at hand every day of our life and available to anyone who sees with faith and listens with love? God is true to the divine promise of presence and makes it possible for us to move beyond the reports from others to the point of giving our own testimony. We can all sing — alleluia — because Christ is present in word and sacrament and community. Nor is this just hearsay.

- *How much of your knowledge of God is hearsay?*

- *When have you been touched by Mystery?*

- *In speaking of God, complete the sentence: "I say..."*

Praying with the Church

> God of power and mercy,
> send your Holy Spirit
> to live in our hearts
> and make us temples of his glory.
> We ask this through our Lord Jesus Christ, your Son,
> who lives and reigns with you and the Holy Spirit,
> one God, for ever and ever.

WEDNESDAY of the SEVENTH WEEK of EASTER
John 17:11–19

THE PRAYER OF JESUS is filled with wild hope. He is confident that the Father will protect his disciples, keep them from harm, and consecrate them in truth. The whole tone of the prayer is permeated with trust and deep reliance on God's saving providence. Though Jesus was aware that his own journey would soon be over, his concern was for the well-being of his followers. With supreme confidence Jesus knew that the Father would bring to fulfillment the wild hope of the kingdom in all those who followed the Son.

Refrain: Thanks be to God who has given us the victory through our Lord Jesus Christ, alleluia.

WILD HOPES

"But in fact how many of us are genuinely moved in the depth of our hearts by the wild hope that our *earth will be recast?"*

Pierre Teilhard de Chardin

Do you have any wild hopes,
or tame ones for that matter?
The possibility of acorns becoming towering oaks,
or caterpillars blossoming into butterflies,
or that dawn will chase away midnight fears?
Wild hopes!
That all creation will learn the dance of joy,
and all humanity might taste the wine of peace,
and that our loving God will become transparent through love.

"Recast the earth, O Lord,
and move our hearts with wild hopes."

Robert F. Morneau

Many of our tame hopes are fulfilled on a daily basis: the hope that the sun will shine, or that the pay check will arrive as planned, or that we will get sufficient nourishment for the day. Though one is disappointed once in awhile, our anticipation of these "small" things, though not insignificant, is frequently realized.

By contrast, some of these same issues for people in other cultures are "wild" hopes. Many of our sisters and brothers do not receive a salary nor do they get three meals a day nor does the sun of freedom shine in their lives. Born into poverty or oppressed by social systems, these people find little joy and peace. If they are fortunate in avoiding violence they still must struggle with resentment and bitterness in their awareness of the consumption and materialism of the wealthy.

We must pray like Jesus that hope might be restored and that the earth might be recast. Only the gift of the Holy Spirit can empower us to trust in the future and to assume our rightful responsibility for the common good. Renewing the face of the earth is the work of the Holy Spirit through those people who say yes to being the Spirit's agents of knowledge, love, and kindness. Our hope, wild or tame, is grounded in God's promise of presence. Herein is our joy and peace.

- *What are two of your wild hopes? Tame hopes?*

- *What are you doing in the field of ecology to renew the face of the earth?*

- *How do you deal with discouragement and depression — the absence of hope?*

Praying with the Church

> God of mercy,
> unite your Church in the Holy Spirit
> that we may serve you with all our hearts
> and work together with unselfish love.
> Grant this through our Lord Jesus Christ, your Son,
> who lives and reigns with you and the Holy Spirit,
> one God, for ever and ever.

THURSDAY of the SEVENTH WEEK of EASTER
John 17:20–26

I N THE CENTER of the mystery of God is oneness, a profound unity of Father, Son, and Spirit. We humans are made
in the image of God and are called to be one within ourselves
and among ourselves. Facts prove to the contrary. We are di-
vided within and feel alienation, the effect of sin. So Jesus,
united to the Father and the Spirit of love, prays that the disciples and all people might be true to their identity and live a
godlike life.

*Refrain: Go into the world and teach all nations. Baptize them in the
name of the Father and of the Son and of the Holy Spirit, alleluia.*

THE TRINITY

Can a doctrine be a companion on life's journey,
say, the belief in the Trinity?
Can one carry in one's heart one substance
along with three "persons" and things like
generation and procession and spiration?
Ancient categories confuse the contemporary mind
causing us to lose unity in diversity, distinctness in uniformity.
The poverty of language urges us to silence
yet experience pushes us to speak even if only to stutter.
To taste creative energy in the rising sun,
to be touched by an incarnate presence at noon,
to be drawn and guided in love even as evening falls
— ah, we must speak of light and love and life.

If the word "God" is too small
let us use "Trinity" to catch it all,
all the beauty that we call radiant glory.

Robert F. Morneau

Traveling alone is not wise. So we look for companions to keep us company and to share the joys and hardships of our pilgrim way. Breaking bread and sharing wine with friends are special graces for the journey. But then we are also blessed by being given truths, truths that nourish our mind and fuel our decisions. One such revelation we call the Trinity, the belief in one God, three persons. This company gives us wisdom because it tells us who we are.

Jesus lives in relationship to his Father and together they share the Spirit of love. This community of persons in one Godhead is so mysterious that our finite minds and hearts must try to yield to appreciation rather than comprehension. We are not masters of mystery but servants and agents of it. Our knowledge of the Trinity will come more in living a Trinitarian life than attempting to gain theological knowledge of it.

There are two practices that make the companionship of this doctrine of the Trinity a constant in our lives: making the sign of the cross and saying "Glory be to the Father and to the Son and to the Holy Spirit." In both this sign and in these words we have the opportunity of "touching" the mystery time after time. But two things are necessary: deep faith and reverence. We sign ourselves with care and we speak the "Glory be..." from the heart. And God is with us.

- *Who are your companions? People? Truths?*

- *Do you make the sign of the cross with meaning and reverence?*

- *Why are the mysteries of the Trinity and the incarnation the pillars of Christianity?*

Praying with the Church

> Father,
> let your Spirit come upon us with power
> to fill us with his gifts.
> May he make our hearts pleasing to you,
> and ready to do your will.
> We ask this through our Lord Jesus Christ, your Son,
> who lives and reigns with you and the Holy Spirit,
> one God, forever and ever.

FRIDAY of the SEVENTH WEEK of EASTER
John 21:15–19

THERE IS A DEEP TENSION within the human heart between doing our own will ("willfulness") and surrendering to a direction not of our own design ("willingness"). Jesus is honest with Peter: if you "follow me," you will not be your own master. Peter is direct with Jesus: I do love you and will continue your mission of caring for people. Though the protestation is strong we know that the struggle continues through life between doing it "my way" and "your will be done."

Refrain: Jesus Christ died and is risen from the dead. Now he lives forever at the right hand of the Father where he intercedes for us, alleluia.

"In God We Trust"

The currency is clear in its claim:
the Deity the object of trust.
But then the haggling begins:
    would not golden calves outweigh burdensome etched
        stones?
    would not the immediacy of pleasure supplant eternal
        promises?
    would not a bird in our earthly hand be better than two
        in a heavenly bush?
Yet the coin is clear in its claim: "In God We Trust!"

I was too young to know it was a wooden nickel!

Robert F. Morneau

Trust is one of the foundational virtues of the spiritual life, like its cousins gratitude and generosity. God makes and keeps promises and we can rely on the divine word. Peter was well aware that without divine grace he would slip back into betrayal and infidelity. His hope was not in his own strength but in the person of Jesus and the power of the Holy Spirit.

But there are other hopes in other things. Golden calves come in many forms: a huge financial portfolio, houses too big for the filling, power amassed and not shared. Another contemporary hope is pleasure and avoidance of all pain. The pleasure principle has become the only standard for much of modern morality. And then we hedge our bet by putting stock in the here and now with no thought to the future, to that strange land of eschatology, the last things. Trust can go in many directions.

Wooden nickels do not do well in the marketplace. They cannot even purchase a gum ball. Real nickels can do that and remind us, if we are attentive, that it is in God that our trust lies. No matter that current philosophies try to deface the coin. Even if they were successful in such an enterprise, the words are still embedded along the bottom of the soul, and no philosophy or strange theology can eradicate them.

- *Who were the teachers who taught you to trust?*

- *How did you react the first time people broke their trust? The first time you broke your trust?*

- *Do you have wooden nickels or real ones in your pocket?*

Praying with the Church

> Father,
> in glorifying Christ and sending us your Spirit,
> you open the way to eternal life.
> May our sharing in this gift increase our love
> and make our faith grow stronger.
> Grant this through our Lord Jesus Christ, your Son,
> who lives and reigns with you and the Holy Spirit,
> one God, for ever and ever.

SATURDAY of the SEVENTH WEEK of EASTER
John 21:20–25

K NOWING WHAT ONE'S BUSINESS IS and what should not be major concerns are two significant graces. Peter's business was to follow the Lord, not to know how the Lord would work in the lives of his fellow disciples. When we respond to what the Lord asks of us, each in our own unique circumstances and according to our own gifts, we give testimony to God and further the kingdom. Each of us is asked to add just one page to the great volume of salvation history.

Refrain: Know that I am with you always, even until the end of the world, alleluia.

EASTER VIGIL

We know how to do it right:
scatter the old darkness with a new fire;
fill the silence with stories
of creation, redemption, liberation;
throw fresh water on parched lives;
anoint with oil the sheep the shepherd calls home;
break the bread lest souls remain dead;
shout alleluias into an empty tomb.

Now we can say

"O happy fault, O necessary evil"

that merited such a redeemer.

Robert F. Morneau

One of the most important businesses of the Church is liturgy, our public worship. And within that vocation one of the most important moments is the Easter Vigil when we gather to celebrate our liberation from sin and death. Were it not in the official, approved liturgy of the Church, we might be tempted to call heretical this claim that the sin of the Adam was *felix culpa* — "a happy fault." Yet our faith is deep enough to do just that. More, our faith perceives Jesus as the one who came to conquer sin and death.

Our lives are about fire, the Easter fire. Peter and John were given the flame of the Holy Spirit and they scattered the darkness of their time by their teaching and witness. We are given the same task: to be on fire with the love of God and to continue to tell the story of God's saving presence. Our vocation is to grow in holiness, perfecting love by giving it away.

In the end the tomb is empty. Because of Jesus we can shout our alleluias even in the face of death. Every time we break the bread we reexperience the paschal mystery and are drawn more deeply into the life of the Spirit. If sin was a necessary evil then grace is our extravagant good.

- *Are you comfortable with the expression "O happy fault" as applied to sin?*

- *What meaning does the Easter Vigil hold for you?*

- *Is "your business" to follow in the way of the Lord?*

Praying with the Church

Almighty Father,
let the love we have celebrated in this Easter season
be put into practice in our daily lives.

We ask this through our Lord Jesus Christ, your Son,
who lives and reigns with you and the Holy Spirit,
one God, for ever and ever.

PENTECOST SUNDAY
John 20:19–23

THE JOURNEY FROM EASTER TO PENTECOST cannot be measured either by miles or time. Though some seven weeks of the calendar have past, the mystery of Jesus' rising and the coming of the Holy Spirit in fire and wind cannot be held in time/space categories. We are in the land of faith; we dwell in the geography of mystery. It all speaks of one thing: life, our life in a God who not only creates us but redeems us through the Son's death and resurrection and who continues to lead and guide us still through the wisdom and power of the Holy Spirit. Grace is the gift of God's very self to humankind.

Refrain: Receive the Holy Spirit; the sins of those you forgive shall be forgiven, alleluia.

GLORY

How to name God's weighty radiance!
Light shining in our troubled world's darkness?
A cloud guiding and freeing us every step of the way?
A fire of love pillaring us through the night?

God's glory? Just ask St. Irenaeus:
    "...the human person fully alive..."

God's greater glory? St. Ignatius' life's dream:
"Ad majorem Dei gloriam!"
God's greatest glory? Ask any child:
"Love and be loved!"

Robert F. Morneau

"The world will be saved by beauty" (Dostoevsky). Novelists and poets use a different language system than theologians. We know that the world is saved through the redemptive sacrifice of Jesus, but what is this, if not a thing of great beauty, of great glory? Pentecost is the feast of beauty and glory for it brings to full light the radiance of God's love. The Spirit of the Father and the Son is poured out upon all who open their hearts to the truth and seek to do good. The Spirit continues to breathe life and grace into creation.

"Glory" is an illusive term, but it is not an abstract reality. Glory is experienced when the brilliant sunrise scatters the darkness of night, when a child is born in Bethlehem and hope surges through the land, when people enter into serious conversation in search of truth, when justice breaks the chain of oppression. Glory is all around us if we have eyes to see and ears to hear. Glory happens when love is given and received.

Pentecost is the feast of freedom. With the descent of the Holy Spirit those who had lost hope now have courage. Fear no longer holds in bondage those who would be disciples of the risen Lord. The Spirit sets us free to worship the Lord in holiness and justice. Our task is to be open to the fire. Our task is then to share the gifts given to us.

- *When have you experienced "glory"?*
- *How does the Holy Spirit work in your life?*
- *How do you celebrate the great feasts of Christmas, Easter, Pentecost?*

Praying with the Church

Father of light, from whom every good gift comes,
send your Spirit into our lives
with the power of a mighty wind,
and by the flame of your wisdom
open the horizons of our minds.
Loosen our tongues to sing your praise
in words beyond the power of speech,
for without your Spirit
man could never raise his voice in words of peace
or announce the truth that Jesus is Lord,
who lives and reigns with you and the Holy Spirit,
one God, for ever and ever.

Epilogue

As we leave the Easter Season and enter "ordinary time," our spiritual hungers remain. It seems appropriate, therefore, to suggest various poetic resources that might enrich our minds and hearts in seasons other than "high" liturgical celebration such as Advent, Lent, and Easter/Pentecost. Here are five recommended texts for one's bookbag.

The Enlightened Heart: An Anthology of Sacred Poetry, edited by Stephen Mitchell (New York: Harper & Row, Publishers, 1989), 171 pages. Cutting across cultures and religions, this rich volume of verse offers a wide variety of religious experiences as expressed by such poets as Hildegard of Bingen, Francis of Assisi, Rumi, Dante, Mirabai, George Herbert, William Blake, Yeats, Antonio Machado, Rainer Maria Rilke. In simple and complex language, in images at times clear and sometimes obscure, we are given a wide range of perspectives on divine transcendence. A treasure trove here.

The New Oxford Book of Christian Verse, chosen and edited by Donald Davie (New York: Oxford University Press, 1981), 320 pages. This volume takes us on a long poetic journey of religious verse in the English-speaking world. The reader meets along the road to Emmaus or London, Chicago or Brisbane, such poets as Chaucer, John Donne, John Milton, Henry Vaughan, Thomas Traherne, Charles Wesley, Emily Dickinson, Christina Rossetti, and many more. These individuals had a vision of the divine and the skill to share their experience. An enriching text.

David Whyte's *The Heart Aroused: Poetry and the Preservation of the Soul in Corporate America* (New York: Doubleday, 1994), 323 pages. The danger of losing one's soul, whether to the company store or simply to an age of consumeristic materialism, is an abiding concern. How can we preserve our soul and foster its growth in such an environment? Music and art will help, as will a life of prayer, discipline, and generosity. And then there is poetry, a type of discourse that rouses the heart to the deeper mysteries of life. If we live on images, then we must nourish the growth of our religious imagination, and poetry is primary source for this development.

Poems and Prose of Gerard Manley Hopkins, selected with an introduction by W. H. Gardner (Baltimore: Penguin Books, 1953), 252 pages. If setting off for the proverbial island with only three books allowed in my bookbag, surely there would be the Bible, Shakespeare, and a volume of Hopkins's verse. A single poem of this great poet, be it "God's Grandeur" or "Pied Beauty" or "Hurrahing in Harvest," can nourish the heart for many moons. Even a single line will do it: "There lives the dearest freshness deep down things."

Poems of R. S. Thomas (Fayetteville: University of Arkansas Press, 1983), 196 pages. Welsh poet R. S. Thomas, one of those struggling pilgrims who is not afraid to raise the large metaphysical questions and face the dark side of life, speaks from the heart and invites the reader of his verse to ponder deeply the mystery of existence. A prayerful reading of "The Kingdom," "The Moor," "Poetry for Supper," "The Presence," and "There" will enrich the human journey.

And don't forget to throw in your bookbag Mary Oliver's *New and Selected Poems* (Boston: Beacon Press, 1992) and Wislawa Szymborska's *View with a Grain of Sand: Selected Poems* (New York: Harcourt Brace & Company, 1993) and *The Essential Rumi* (Edison, N.J.: Castle Books, 1997) and *Times Alone: Selected Poems of Antonio Machado* (Middletown, Conn.: Wesleyan University Press, 1983) and *The Complete Poems of Emily Dickinson* and ... and ... and ... and ...